SKIP THE DRAMA

SKIP THE
DRAMA

PRACTICAL, GET-AHEAD STRATEGIES TO SURVIVE YOUR DAUGHTER'S TEENAGE YEARS

DR SARAH HUGHES

EXISLE
PUBLISHING

First published 2018
Exisle Publishing Pty Ltd
PO Box 864, Chatswood, NSW 2057, Australia
226 High Street, Dunedin, 9016, New Zealand
www.exislepublishing.com

A CiP record for this book is available from the National Library of Australia.

ISBN 978-1-925335-85-9

Designed by Sarah Anderson
Typeset in Adobe Garamond 11 pt
Printed in China

This book uses paper sourced under ISO 14001 guidelines from well-managed forests and other controlled sources.

10 9 8 7 6 5 4 3 2 1

Disclaimer
This book is a general guide only and should never be a substitute for the skill, knowledge and experience of a qualified medical professional dealing with the facts, circumstances and symptoms of a particular case. The nutritional, medical and health information presented in this book is based on the research, training and professional experience of the author, and is true and complete to the best of their knowledge. However, this book is intended only as an informative guide; it is not intended to replace or countermand the advice given by the reader's personal physician. Because each person and situation is unique, the author and the publisher urge the reader to check with a qualified healthcare professional before using any procedure where there is a question as to its appropriateness. The author, publisher and their distributors are not responsible for any adverse effects or consequences resulting from the use of the information in this book. It is the responsibility of the reader to consult a physician or other qualified healthcare professional regarding their personal care. This book contains references to products that may not be available everywhere. The intent of the information provided is to be helpful; however, there is no guarantee of results associated with the information provided.

Dr Sarah Hughes completed her clinical training at the University of Sydney and holds a Doctorate in Clinical Psychology and a PhD in child and adolescent anxiety disorders. Sarah is the founder of Think Clinical Psychologists, and has ten years of clinical experience.

CONTENTS

INTRODUCTION

When your daughter enters her teenage years there's a definite shift. The easygoing pre-teen who once enjoyed your company and happily complied with your requests now has to be bribed to grace you with her presence, and can't do anything you ask without questioning it first. Household peace is broken over arguments about her excessive phone use, poor time management and lax approach to curfew, not to mention the debates that start over her selfish demands, routine thoughtlessness and general lack of respect for the people around her.

And if that's not enough to push you to your limit, with current mental health statistics being what they are — some studies show that as many as one in five teens struggle with mental health issues — odds are that at some point in her teenage years you'll be caught off-guard by an eating disorder, anxiety, or depression, with cutting thrown in for good measure, just to really keep things interesting.

Parenting has always been a tough gig, but parenting a teenage daughter in today's world is a uniquely stressful experience, and one which leaves most parents — even the most resilient ones — feeling beaten, frazzled and confused. The right strategies, executed correctly, are the key to your survival, and the good news is, no matter the issue, this book has you covered.

Over my years of practice as a clinical psychologist I've worked with hundreds of families and teenage girls. They all struggle with similar issues and it's what motivated me to write this book. You'll see in most chapters I've included case studies to give voice to a particular issue; but while it might seem like I'm talking about a specific teen or family, each case study is actually just a hypothetical example based on work I've done with families over the years.

If your daughter's teenage years have started and you're already at your wits' end, regain your sanity and use the strategies in this book to turn things around. If you've had a dream run so far and your teen is for the most part charming and agreeable, thank your lucky stars but don't get complacent. All teens need help if they're going to develop into well-adjusted, respectful and self-sufficient young adults, and the advice in this book will make you a better teacher. And if you've got a few years up your sleeve before you hit the adolescent runway — get a step ahead. Set yourself up for a smooth transition into her teenage years by implementing the right strategies now. When your relationship survives the onslaught of adolescence and you skip the drama, you'll be glad you did.

Let's get started.

1

WHEN YOUR DAUGHTER'S SELFISH

Teens are, in general, inherently self-focused. They think about their own needs and wants first and rarely stop to consider how their actions affect the people around them. Understandably, it's a trait that makes them wildly unpopular with parents and siblings alike. It's frustrating to live with someone who doesn't think to clean up after themselves, who expects their needs for lifts and money to be met at the last minute and without warning, and who shows no appreciation or awareness for the sacrifices others make to meet their needs.

I've lost count of the number of parents I've worked with, like Sam below, who are left floored by the level of their teenage daughter's selfishness.

I don't know how we got here. Lauren used to be such a sweet and kind-hearted little girl. She had such beautiful manners and was always so thoughtful, picking me flowers from the garden and giving me hugs when I looked tired after a long day at work. Now she barely acknowledges me — unless, of course, she wants something — and thinks I'm subjecting her to forced labour when I ask her to put her dirty dishes in the dishwasher. They're her dishes! I'm not asking her to pick up after anyone else!

Last week she called me from school, hysterical, because she'd forgotten an assignment. She was absolutely beside herself, so I rescheduled a work meeting, raced home to grab her assignment, then drove like a maniac to get it to her by her lunchtime deadline. She didn't even say thank you. She barely grunted at me when I got to the school gates, and when she got home from school, there was no mention of the assignment at all.

The only interaction we had that night was over a new pair of shoes I'd bought. Can you believe she reprimanded me for spending money? She was annoyed that I'd bought myself a new pair of shoes when I'd refused to give her money to see a movie at the weekend. And the worst part is, she wasn't kidding! She genuinely thought it was unfair that I'd used *my* money to buy myself something nice without offering her money for something as well.

It's like she thinks we've all been put on this earth to serve her. It's so frustrating! I've tried again and again to talk to her about her attitude, but nothing I say seems to make an ounce of difference. It makes me cringe when I think about how selfish she's become.

Just like Lauren, most teens take more than they give and tend not to appreciate the unreasonableness of their demands. But as infuriating as their selfishness is — and it is hugely infuriating — it's not necessarily deliberate. In fact, a growing body of research supports the idea that your daughter's self-centredness isn't a personality flaw like you might at first think. According to science, your daughter's selfishness is a symptom of her still-developing adolescent brain.

Selfish behaviour and the teenage brain

During the first few years of life, the brain grows rapidly and several hundred new neural connections are formed every second. After this period of rapid growth, the brain changes to become more efficient, via a process called synaptic pruning. Synaptic pruning finetunes our neural circuitry based on our experiences and our neural history: frequently used neural connections are preserved and strengthened, and connections that are rarely used are pruned away to make way for new growth. The strengthening of neural connections due to activity is what's behind neural plasticity — the ability of our brain to adapt and change itself in response to our experiences.

We used to think that very little change occurred in the brain after the first few years of life, but a huge amount has been discovered in the last decade about the changes that occur in the brain throughout adolescence. One of the most important findings from recent research is that the brain actually undergoes a second period of synaptic pruning in the teenage years. We've also learnt that over the course of adolescence, different areas of the brain undergo development at different times. In short, areas of the brain responsible for more basic functions — like motor control or sensory processing — undergo development first, and areas responsible for more complex skills and functions mature last.

One of the last regions of the brain to mature is the prefrontal cortex. It's an important area of the brain and is responsible for a number of different cognitive functions. It's involved in everything from planning, emotional and behavioural control, to problem-solving and decision-making. The prefrontal cortex also plays an important role in helping us to understand the perspectives of other people, one of the key skills your teen needs in order to be less selfish. What's interesting is that not only do adults and teens have structurally different prefrontal cortices, researchers have also found that adults and teens use different areas of the prefrontal cortex when they're completing tasks that require them to think about the thoughts and feelings of other people. What this seems to suggest is that as the brain develops, the way in which we make social decisions changes too.

Knowledge that the brain continues to undergo significant change throughout adolescence has led researchers to try to understand typical teenage behaviours — like self-centredness, heightened risk-taking and impulsiveness — in relation to the structural changes occurring in the teenage brain. At the forefront of research in this area is Sarah-Jayne Blakemore, a professor and lead researcher at the University College London Institute of Cognitive Neuroscience. One area Professor Blakemore is particularly interested in is how the development of the prefrontal cortex affects the ability of teens to understand and make inferences about the thoughts and feelings of others. To this end, she and her research team use brain scans and computerized tasks to compare the performance of adults and teens on tasks which test perspective-taking skills.

One of the tasks they use is the director task, seen in Figure 1 (opposite). In this task, participants are shown a bookshelf filled with objects. As you can see in Figure 1, some objects are visible from both the front and back of the bookshelf, while some can only be seen from the front; the back view of these objects is blocked by panels on the back of the bookshelf as seen in Figure 2 (opposite). Participants are asked to move objects on the bookshelf to different positions in one of two ways. Some participants are asked to ignore objects on those shelves with a back panel and only move objects on the open shelves. Other participants are given an instruction by a director — a person standing behind the bookshelf. How the instructions are delivered is important, because participants following instructions from the director have a

FIGURE 1: YOUR VIEW

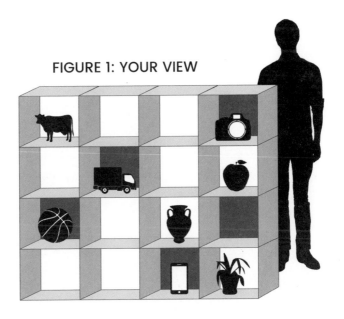

FIGURE 2: DIRECTOR'S VIEW

Images from a computerized task used in studies conducted by Professor Blakemore.

harder task; they have to remember to take the director's perspective into account before deciding which objects to move (i.e. the director isn't going to ask participants to move objects he can't see).

The results of this study were interesting. What Professor Blakemore and her team found is that when teenagers and adults don't have to take the perspective of a director into account, they perform equally well. But when participants do have to remember to take the perspective of the director into account, teens struggle with this condition and make significantly more errors than adults.[1] This is important, because it suggests that teens aren't as able as adults to consider the perspective of another person, probably because the area of their brain that supports this skill, the prefrontal cortex, is still developing.

What all of the above findings tell us is that the teenage brain is still maturing. It continues to undergo significant change right throughout adolescence and the result of this is lagging skills in certain areas, like the ability to consider the thoughts and feelings of others. The good news? Your daughter's selfishness isn't set in stone just yet. With a little bit of help, she can still learn to be less self-focused.

Teach your teen to be less selfish

The second phase of synaptic pruning that takes place throughout adolescence means your daughter's brain is particularly plastic: it's ready and able to change in response to new experiences, heightening her capacity for learning. When she practises new skills, new neural pathways are forged and strengthened, and these physical changes enhance her skill development. Use this to your advantage. Teach her to be less selfish by helping her to practise the skills she needs to be more thoughtful and considerate.

How you respond to your daughter's selfishness can either help or hinder her skill development. Take Lauren's mother Sam, for example.

Sam is understandably frustrated. Lauren is behaving like an ungrateful, self-centred brat but, to be fair, Sam isn't entirely blameless. Sam might think she's teaching Lauren that her selfishness is unacceptable, but her actions are at odds with her lectures. Lauren's given most things she wants without having to do much in return. If she wants new clothes, she only has to send Mum a link to the new dress she's got her eye on. If she needs a lift, someone's always free to take her. And if she forgets something she needs — a school assignment, lunch, her sports uniform — Sam puts her own life on hold and bends over backwards to lend a helping hand.

Sam wants to give Lauren all the things she didn't have growing up — attention, respect, unconditional love and parental support — but she's giving too much. She hardly ever says no, and she continues to give, even when Lauren's giving her nothing back in return. Lauren doesn't think about how her actions affect other people because she doesn't have to. Sam might reprimand her for her complete disregard for other people's time and effort on a regular basis, but because Lauren continues to get what she wants regardless, Sam's words don't carry much weight. Fact is, Sam's actions are reinforcing Lauren's thoughtlessness and if things don't change, there's a fair chance Lauren's selfishness will only get worse.

Build thoughtfulness by encouraging self-reflection

Don't fall into Sam's trap. Encourage your daughter to be less selfish by helping her to practise taking other people's thoughts and needs into consideration. Start by helping her to be more aware of how her actions affect the people around her. It will be easy to think of examples that relate to family life, but your daughter is more likely to be worried about the impact of her behaviour on her friendships, so for effectiveness' sake, start here. When you see your daughter forgetting to take the thoughts and feelings of her friends into account — for example, if you notice she isn't pulling her weight in a group assignment, or if she cancels plans with one friend because she's had a better offer from someone else — encourage her to stop and think about how her actions might be affecting the people around her. To be effective, you'll need to be neutral in your approach. If she senses your judgment, her anger will inhibit self-reflection, so avoid accusatory statements like, 'Don't you think it's a bit selfish to cancel your plans with Madeleine just so you can spend time with Amanda?' and instead ask general, open-ended questions like, 'How does Madeleine feel about that?' If you're met with a response like 'she's fine with it', let it be. The more you argue with your daughter the more indignant she'll become, and this will affect her ability to step back and see the situation from a different point of view. Plant the seed by raising the question and leave your daughter to reflect more on this in her own time.

Stop saying yes to selfish requests

Your teen will also benefit from hearing the word 'no' when she makes a selfish request. Say your teen comes to you and wants to be driven to a friend's house after lunch. You have a laundry list of jobs to do around the house and you'd also hoped to get out for a coffee with a friend. You're frustrated your teen hasn't given you more notice and annoyed that she has the audacity to ask for a lift, especially given you spent all day yesterday chauffeuring her around to various sporting and social commitments. You lecture her about the disruptiveness of her last-minute planning, and vent about her lack of consideration for others — but because you end up driving her anyway, none of this sinks in. Worse, because you've altered your plans to accommodate hers, you inadvertently reinforce her selfishness. You teach her that her needs are a priority and far more important than yours: why else would you re-arrange your day to meet her request?

If her requests are selfish, say no. It won't kill her, I promise.

Teach consideration by saying, 'Yes, if ...'

How you respond to your teen's request for favours is important. She'll only learn to think about how her behaviour affects other people if she receives meaningful feedback from you. If your daughter's needs are met without any sacrifice on her behalf, it doesn't matter how many lectures you give, she won't develop the skills she needs to take your thoughts and feelings into consideration, because your words don't match your actions. Your lectures tell her that her actions are ill considered, but your actions tell her that her needs are your priority.

To teach your teen to be less selfish, you need to start putting your needs on the table in a practical way. When a situation arises that requires you to modify your plans to meet your daughter's needs, make your 'yes' conditional. Agree to drive her to her friend's house, for example, but on terms that are agreeable to you. Think about what you need from her to feel happy about accommodating her request, and negotiate. Using the example above, this might look something like, 'I'm happy to take you to Olivia's house, but there are things I need to get done around the house today. I'll need your help with some of these tasks if I'm going to have time to drive you there and pick you up later. I need to hang out the washing, unpack the dishwater, fold the laundry and clean the bathroom. What can you help me with to free up the hour I'll need to drive you?'

A conditional yes will help your teen start to think about other people and slowly break her out of her 'me, me, me' mindset. Because a conditional yes also helps to recalibrate the give-and-take in your relationship, you might also find that this strategy helps you let go of some of the frustration you've been feeling towards your teen. But as effective as a conditional yes can be, bear in mind that if you've said yes unconditionally up to this point, it might take your teen some time to adjust to the new state of play. She may initially decide she'd rather retract her request than meet you halfway, and if she does, respect her choice and don't get drawn into an argument. Give yourself permission to stick to your conditions and remind her that you're happy to help if she changes her mind. Remember, taking other people's thoughts and feelings into consideration is a skill she's still developing, and practice makes perfect.

The important bits

+ The ability to take other people's thoughts and feelings into consideration is a skill still developing in adolescents.
+ The teenage brain is plastic, meaning it can change to support the learning of new skills, including social skills like perspective-taking.
+ DO help your daughter to be more aware of how her actions affect the people around her by asking non-judgmental, open-ended questions.
+ DON'T accuse your teen of being selfish. Remember, self-centred thinking is a symptom of her neuroanatomy, not a trait of her personality.
+ DO help your teen to be more aware of how her requests impact the family by putting your needs on the table.
+ DON'T give in to selfish requests or you may inadvertently reinforce selfish behaviour.
+ DON'T rely on lectures to teach your teen to be less self-focused.
+ DO attach conditions when you say yes, to motivate your teen to consider the impact of her requests.

2

WHEN YOUR DAUGHTER'S A PROCRASTINATOR

It's frustrating to watch your teen make the same mistake over and over again, such as when she repeatedly puts off tasks and ends up in a panic when she realizes how much work she has to do and how little time she has to do it. The pattern is always the same. She stays up late to complete homework she could have started earlier, and her assignments are finished in a frantic last-minute rush the night before they're due. In between tears and her desperate pleas for help, she promises to start tasks earlier in the future, but she never seems to learn from her mistakes. She knows all the reasons why she shouldn't leave things to the last minute, yet she falls into the same procrastination trap each and every time. Her life is a series of panicked, rushed attempts to get things done, which is stressful for her and exhausting for you. So how do you break the cycle?

If your daughter procrastinates, it's not because she's lazy. Her tendency to leave things to the last minute might make you question her level of motivation, but procrastination is often a symptom of other underlying issues, the main culprits being a need for control, anxiety, and poor organizational skills.

Why do teens procrastinate?

There are three main types of teenage procrastinators. Your daughter might fit clearly into one category or she might be a mixed procrastinator and tick multiple boxes.

The need-for-control procrastinator

These teens are sensitive to being controlled and resent having tasks imposed upon them by others. As their name suggests, the need-for-control procrastinator delays starting tasks to take back control.

The anxious procrastinator

There are two types of anxious procrastinators: perfectionistic procrastinators and easily-overwhelmed procrastinators. Perfectionistic procrastinators procrastinate because they're overwhelmed by the pressure to excel academically. Easily-overwhelmed procrastinators are easily overwhelmed when it comes to academic pressure. They procrastinate to avoid the anxiety school work triggers.

The poorly-organized procrastinator

Poorly-organized procrastinators lack the skills they need to plan ahead and stay on task. Their procrastination is due to a skills deficit, not laziness.

Knowing your daughter's procrastination type is essential. If you don't understand the driving force behind her procrastination, you won't be able to help her break her procrastination habit. Use the information below to help you figure out her procrastination style. Let's look at each of these types of procrastinator in a little more detail.

The need-for-control procrastinator

Throughout adolescence, teens develop a stronger sense of self, and with this comes both a desire for more freedom and an acute sensitivity to the feeling of being controlled. Some teens see homework as a violation of their right to be in control of their own life, and this drives their resistance to homework and their propensity to procrastinate over assignments and study. To the need-for-control procrastinator, starting tasks ahead of time isn't a course of action that helps their own interest; it's an intolerable concession of control and procrastination helps them to save face.

The anxious procrastinator

Anxiety is another common cause of procrastination in teens. The two most common types of anxious procrastinators are perfectionistic procrastinators and easily-overwhelmed procrastinators. Perfectionistic procrastinators place undue pressure on themselves to excel academically and procrastinate to delay evaluation by others. Easily-overwhelmed procrastinators, on the other hand, have a lower threshold for stress and are more vulnerable to stress and anxiety in the face of multiple assessments and overlapping deadlines.

Like perfectionistic procrastinators, easily-overwhelmed procrastinators procrastinate to avoid the stress and anxiety that school work triggers. But while procrastination offers relief from stress and anxiety in the short-term, it causes more stress longer-term as work builds up and deadlines multiply. It might seem counterintuitive to rely on a strategy that ultimately makes things worse, but anxiety isn't logical. Anxious teens are motivated by a desire to feel less anxious, and the short-term relief that procrastination offers is what entices perfectionistic procrastinators and easily-overwhelmed procrastinators to procrastinate.

The poorly-organized procrastinator

There's evidence to suggest that some teens procrastinate because their developing brains can't yet support the cognitive skills they need to self-regulate and stay on task. The brain changes over adolescence. It rewires itself for faster and more efficient synaptic communication, but different parts of the brain are rewired at different times according to a pre-determined schedule of development. One of the last regions to mature is the prefrontal cortex, a part of the brain responsible for the cognitive skills your teen needs to be organized and stay on task. Her procrastination might seem deliberate, but this isn't necessarily the case. The inability of poorly-organized procrastinators to plan ahead and meet deadlines may actually be a symptom of them not yet having the neural scaffolding they need to be proactive and task-focused.

If your daughter's a poorly-organized procrastinator, her procrastination should reduce over time as her brain develops, but the brain is also incredibly plastic and has the ability to change itself to support the learning of new skills. So the good news is, your daughter doesn't have to wait for her prefrontal cortex to be remodelled to break free of her procrastination cycle. She can speed up the rewiring of her brain by learning and practising new skills for organization.

Breaking the procrastination cycle: bridging the skills gap

If it was as simple as choosing not to procrastinate, your teen would have done that by now. Threatening consequences and offering rewards also won't work, because motivation isn't the issue — skills are.

Your daughter is missing the key skills she needs to break free of her procrastination. Need-for-control procrastinators lack the skills they need to complete tasks others have asked them do; anxious procrastinators are missing the skills they need to better manage their anxiety; and poorly-organized procrastinators are lacking when it comes to organizational skills.

Staying up late to help your daughter finish work she's left to the last minute or emailing teachers on her behalf to request extensions might help to avoid a meltdown in the short-term, but saving her from the natural consequences of her procrastination is a band-aid solution and it won't help her to do things differently in the future. What your daughter needs is help to learn the missing skills driving her procrastination.

Understanding your daughter's procrastination

To help your daughter break out of her procrastination cycle, you first need to understand the underlying cause of her procrastination. If the skills you try to help her build don't match her procrastination type, your efforts won't be effective. Not only that, if your approach is incompatible with her procrastination type you might inadvertently make things worse. For instance, if your teen procrastinates because she resents having homework forced on her, stepping in to try to help her to be more organized may backfire. She'll see your efforts as an attempt to control her and be even more resistant to starting work as a result.

What's my daughter's procrastination type?

How you support your daughter will depend on the underlying cause of her procrastination. If you're unsure what drives her procrastination, think about how she functions in other areas of her life.

The need-for-control procrastinator: As a general rule, if control is an underlying cause, your teen is more likely to be strong-willed and stubborn in other areas of her life, resistant to your input when it comes to advice-giving, and argumentative when it comes to limit setting.

The anxious procrastinator: If your teen's a worrier, if she's perfectionistic, or if she's easily overwhelmed by stress, then anxiety is a likely cause of her procrastination.

The poorly-organized procrastinator: If poor organization is what's contributing to your daughter's procrastination, she's more likely to struggle with organization in general and be more forgetful than most when it comes to remembering her belongings (e.g. her phone, her bus pass, her textbooks), important dates and appointments.

Helping the need-for-control procrastinator

If control is the issue, you can support your daughter by helping her to see homework as a choice rather than something she has to do. When you talk about homework, choose your words wisely. Ask her what homework she's *going* to do instead of what homework she *has* to do. It might seem like semantics, but language can be powerful. The words you use can be the difference between your teen feeling like she's in control versus feeling like she's being controlled, and the latter may well be what drives her procrastination.

It might also help your daughter to be reminded that whether or not she completes her homework is of no consequence to her teachers. They'll still earn their pay cheque and sleep soundly at night regardless of if she does her homework, but not doing homework will impact her education and the options available to her at the end of her schooling. Don't lecture her, just plant the seed. If her procrastination is a battle for control, the harder you work to get her to see your point of view, the more determined she'll be not to listen.

When control is the issue, less is more.

Helping the anxious procrastinator

If your teen's procrastination is anxiety related, it's important to understand whether she's an easily-overwhelmed procrastinator or a perfectionistic procrastinator.

If she's an easily-overwhelmed procrastinator, breaking assignments down into smaller steps and focusing on one step at a time should help her to feel less stressed. If she feels overwhelmed because she doesn't think she has enough time to get everything done, prioritizing tasks and developing a step-by-step assignment plan with mini-deadlines will also help her to see that her deadlines are achievable. Being able to visualize the completion of tasks will help her to feel less anxious, and this should help to reduce her procrastination.

If your daughter's a perfectionistic procrastinator, she needs your help to re-evaluate her academic standards. This can be a challenge, especially if there's pressure within her school environment to excel academically — which is generally the case in most schools — but re-evaluating her standards is what will help to reduce her reliance on procrastination to cope.

Start by helping your daughter to focus on task completion rather than task performance. You can do this by encouraging her to set process goals (goals that focus on the steps involved in completing a task) rather than outcome-focused goals (goals that focus on marks or ranks). If your daughter has always set outcome-focused goals she might initially find this shift in mindset difficult, but it will be an effective strategy for helping her to manage her anxiety longer-term.

When she finishes an assignment, give your daughter praise for completing the task without the last-minute panic, and avoid inadvertently putting pressure on her to excel with mixed messages. You might tell her that her marks don't matter and her happiness is more important to you than her academic performance, but if you pay more attention to her marks than her other interests, or if you praise her achievements more than her effort, without meaning to you teach her that her academic performance isn't just important, it's the way to earn your approval and affection.

Helping the poorly-organized procrastinator

If your teen leaves tasks to the last minute because she's forgetful and chaotic in her approach to school work, help her to develop the skills she needs to be better organized with her time. Start by helping her put together a timetable that includes time for school work, friends/family, extracurricular activities, exercise, wind-down time and sleep. A timetable will only help if it's something your teen can stick to, so make sure her timetable is realistic and balanced. If your daughter has a large number of extracurricular activities, or if the few extracurricular activities she participates in take up a significant amount of her time, this could be part of the problem. Getting home late and then staying up late to catch up on study might work short-term, but it isn't sustainable long-term and it increases her risk for burn-out and disorganization. If your daughter doesn't have enough time for school work and adequate sleep, look at which extracurricular activities she can drop to make the time.

When it comes to scheduling time for homework, it will be tempting to suggest that your teen starts her homework as soon as she gets home, but this isn't always the right approach. Some teens are most productive when they start work straight away, while others need time to wind down after school and work better after a break. Likewise, whereas some teens work best over longer blocks of time (e.g. two-hour blocks), others are most productive working in 30-minute blocks with ten-minute breaks in between. Your instinct will be to encourage your teen to adopt whatever approach works best for you, but everyone works differently. Be open to helping your daughter to explore what works best for *her*.

Once you have a timetable in place, help your teen develop the skills she needs to be better organized in her approach to school work. Encourage her to get in the habit of writing due dates in her diary and filing assessment notifications where she can easily find them. When she has multiple deadlines, help her to prioritize tasks according to when they're due and how long they'll take to complete.

For larger assignments, help your teen break down the task into smaller steps, and then ask her to estimate how much time she thinks she'll need to complete each step. Use this information to set mini-deadlines, working backwards so she has a clear picture of what needs to get done and by when if she's to successfully finish her assignments on time without the last-minute panic.

One thing to keep in mind is that procrastinators often misjudge how much time they have to get things done and how long tasks will take, so encourage your daughter to be as realistic as possible with time estimates. If she consistently underestimates how much time she needs, encourage her to test her estimates by comparing her predicted completion time with her actual completion time. Doing this should help her learn to be more accurate.

Procrastination skills practice: breaking it down

If your teen's procrastination is driven by lagging organizational skills, breaking tasks into small steps will help her have a clearer picture of exactly what she needs to do to meet a deadline. If anxiety is the underlying cause, breaking tasks down will help large, overwhelming tasks to feel more manageable.

To break an assignment down, help your teen think about the steps she needs to complete to finish her task. Say she has a history essay to write and the guidelines for the essay are quite broad. The task could be broken down into the following steps:

+ Choose a topic.
+ Do general research for my topic.
+ Use my general research to define a specific essay question.
+ Draft a rough essay plan.
+ Expand on my essay plan and list the points I want to cover in each paragraph.
+ Seek guidance and feedback from my history teacher or tutor.
+ Write an introduction.
+ Write paragraphs 1 and 2.
+ Write paragraphs 3 and 4.
+ Write a conclusion.
+ Review and revise my work.
+ Complete a reference list.
+ Print the assignment/upload it for submission.

Putting it into practice

When you start to put things into practice, it'll be tempting to closely supervise your teen's progress to make sure she implements the skills and strategies you've discussed, but be mindful of the difference between supporting her and enabling her by taking on her responsibilities. Whether or not your daughter meets her deadlines is her responsibility. Help her to plan, encourage her to practise skills, and make time to help her if she's asked for help in advance, but don't force compliance or stay up late to help her finish work she should have started earlier. The latter might help your teen to meet her immediate deadline, but it's a band-aid solution and it won't help her to build the skills she needs to stop procrastinating longer-term.

Procrastination apps

If you want to take a step back and let your daughter be responsible for her deadlines, but you're worried she won't stay on track without you, apps are a good middle ground. There are a range of apps designed to help chronic procrastinators to procrastinate less. Each app has a slightly different focus so it's important to pick apps that match your teen's needs, but a couple of good examples are listed for you below.

Todoist: Todoist can help your teen stay on top of her homework and assignments. It allows her to create efficient to-do lists complete with due dates and tasks listed according to their level of priority, making it easy for her to keep track of her deadlines. If large tasks overwhelm her, she can break tasks down into smaller sub-tasks, and best of all the app allows her to send herself task reminders via email or push notifications, which means you can stop monitoring her due dates because the app will do it for you.

Self-control and Freedom: Both of these apps allow users to block any addictive applications that might interfere with productivity for a set period of time. And they mean business. Once you've set your restriction time limits, access to blocked sites is impossible. You can restart your computer or delete the application but it won't matter. The only way to access blocked sites it to wait for the timer to pass. Self-control and Freedom are both great for teens who get distracted by Facebook, Instagram and any other social media platforms when studying.

When things go pear-shaped

Last-minute meltdowns will be the hardest time to not step in, but the same principles apply. If you've had support in place to help your daughter finish her assignment ahead of time but she's chosen to leave things to the last minute, don't step in to help. Saving her won't help her to make a different choice next time, but letting her experience the natural consequences of her procrastination will. Handing in an incomplete assignment or losing marks for handing an assignment in late will be distressing, but it's this distress that will help your daughter to reflect on her actions and acknowledge the need for change. If you help her to finish her assignment, the distress of finishing everything in a mad rush will be overpowered by her relief at getting a completed assignment in on time, and she'll stay stuck in her cycle of procrastination.

What if nothing works?

As with any new skill, your daughter will need time to consolidate the skills she needs to stop procrastinating, but if despite support and natural consequences she continues to struggle to get school work completed, it might be worthwhile investigating whether there are any underlying learning difficulties contributing to the problem. Assessments can be expensive, but if there are attention or learning difficulties at play, you need to know what you're dealing with so you can know how to help. Persistent procrastination might also signal the need for additional support around other underlying causes, such as clinical perfectionism, anxiety disorders and mood-related disorders.

The important bits

+ Procrastination is often a symptom of anxiety, issues relating to control or lagging organizational skills.
+ Understanding why your daughter procrastinates is important. Intervention isn't a one-size-fits-all approach. Your approach will depend on the underlying cause of her procrastination.
+ If she's missing key skills, threats and consequences won't help your daughter to stop procrastinating.
+ DO help your daughter develop the skills she needs to break out of her procrastination cycle, but DON'T enable her procrastination by making her deadlines your responsibility.
+ DO let your teen learn from the natural consequences of her procrastination.
+ If issues with control drive your daughter's procrastination, DO help her to see school work as a choice and not something she's being forced to do.
+ If your daughter is an easily-overwhelmed procrastinator, DO help her to break tasks down into smaller, more manageable steps.
+ If perfectionism is contributing to your daughter's procrastination, DO help her to switch her focus from outcomes to processes.

+ If poor organizational skills are driving your daughter's procrastination, DO help her to be better organized with her time.
+ DO give your teen time to learn the skills she needs to stop procrastinating, but if things don't improve consider seeking additional help.

3

WHEN YOUR DAUGHTER WANTS TO DIET

Each time your daughter goes online, turns on the TV or opens a magazine she's exposed to images and averts that encourage her to diet. Thanks to the multi-billion-dollar diet industry there are literally hundreds of diets for her to choose from: the paleo diet, the vegan diet, low-carb diets, low-fat diets, sugar-free diets, macrobiotic diets, gluten-free diets, raw food diets, the 5:2 diet, the list goes on and on. Given the reach of the diet industry it's in some ways not surprising that most teenage girls diet. What is surprising — and concerning — is that teenage diets are often seen as harmless and dismissed as a passing phase. If you've spent years fighting to get your daughter to eat less junk and more fruit and vegetables, seeing her resolve to eat more healthily might feel like a win, but if your teen does start to show an interest in diets, proceed with caution. Diets can be deceptive.

When healthy eating becomes unhealthy

A resolution to adopt a healthier diet might seem relatively innocuous, but all diets, no matter how healthy, encourage an unhealthy relationship with food. The unhealthy nature of low-calorie diets might be obvious, but diets focused on health and wellbeing also encourage a strict and overly controlled approach to nutrition which can result in teens not eating the nutrients they need.

The motivation for a diet can also quickly shift. What starts as a health kick or a stand against animal cruelty can subtly evolve into something more sinister as food rules multiply and goals change. Take, for example, a teen who stops eating junk food to eat more healthily. Forgoing chips and chocolate might initially be all that's needed to help her to feel better about her diet, but over time her definition of healthy eating may shift to exclude more foods — bread, pasta, dairy, for example — leading her to cut other food groups from her diet as well. The more limited her diet becomes, the more unbalanced her nutrition, and this can start to affect not just her physical health, but her emotional and mental health as well.

Diets will make your daughter feel worse about her body

A large majority of teens — even those already within a healthy weight range — diet to lose weight. They hope that losing weight will help them to feel more body confident, but weight loss-inspired eating is more likely to make your daughter feel worse, not better, about her body.

As soon as she starts dieting to lose weight, there will be a subtle but significant shift in your daughter's food philosophy. Food will stop being a necessary fuel and will become a tool she can use to alter her appearance, and this shift in thinking can be the start of an unhealthy preoccupation with body shape and weight. The more she obsesses over her appearance, the more likely she is to find additional things she dislikes about her body, and her body confidence will start to falter. And while the sense of achievement she feels at the start of a diet might initially boost her body confidence, when she fails to stick to her diet — which at some point she will — or when she doesn't lose weight as quickly as she'd like, she'll judge herself harshly and be critical of not just her lack of willpower, but her body shape and weight as well.

The relationship between diets and eating disorders

The most concerning aspect of dieting behaviour in teens is the relationship between dieting and the development of eating disorders. Eating disorders are complex psychological disorders and we still don't fully understand their etiology. A lot of research has been done to better understand how and why eating disorders develop, and a number of risk factors have been identified as a result. Genetic factors and certain psychological factors like low self-esteem, perfectionism and body image dissatisfaction are all known risks, and we know that exposure to messages — from the media, friends, family — that place an undue emphasis on the importance of being thin puts teens at higher risk as well.

Another key risk factor is dieting. In fact, an important Australian study by Kenardy, Brown and Vogt in 2001 showed that young women who had been on five or more diets in a twelve-month period — classified for the purpose of this study as frequent dieters — were more likely than infrequent and non-dieters to develop eating disorder symptoms. Specifically, frequent dieters were twice as likely to binge eat and four times as likely to purge (use laxatives, diuretics, or self-induced vomiting) to manage their weight. Frequent dieters

29

were also nearly five times more likely to binge *and* purge, and three times more likely to be dissatisfied with their body shape and weight. Interestingly, Kenardy and his colleagues also found that how at-risk participants were for eating disorders was affected by *when* they started dieting. Specifically, young women who dieted before fifteen years of age were twice as likely to report eating disorder behaviours and 70 per cent more likely to be unhappy with their body shape and weight compared to young women who started dieting later in adolescence.[1]

None of the teens I work with set out to develop eating disorders. Most start watching what they eat to be healthier or to lose a small amount of weight, but as their diet gains momentum and their eating becomes more restrictive, they find themselves caught in the early stages of an eating disorder, much like Alison below.

Alison was an outgoing, highly social teen who'd never paid much attention to her diet. Over winter she gained a small amount of weight, so she began exercising more and watching what she ate to get back into shape. Alison's parents were supportive of her health kick at first, but then started to question how healthy her approach to healthy eating really was.

> At first she just stopped eating junk food which we didn't really think too much about, but now she's really fussy about food and we're worried she's getting a bit obsessed with healthy eating. Things she used to love to eat like mashed potato and pasta she won't touch any more; she wants kale chips, cauliflower rice and zucchini pasta instead. As a family we eat pretty healthily anyway — we have stir-frys or chicken and vegetables for dinner

most nights — but she's taking healthy eating to a whole new level, and I think she might be eating less as well.

I know it must sound crazy, us worrying that she's being too healthy, but she's getting more and more strict about what she will and won't eat. She's even started sending me recipes and meal requests! And she's been exercising more, too. She's always played netball or done a team sport, but she asked us for a gym membership for her birthday and she's been running most afternoons after school.

I've tried to talk to her about her diet and exercise, but she rolls her eyes and tells me to stop making a big deal out of nothing. I guess she has a point, it's not like she's stopped eating all together, and I don't think she's lost too much weight, but I can't shake the feeling that something's not right.

Alison's parents are right to be concerned. Alison's health kick might have started innocently enough, but things are starting to shift and Alison's showing early signs of a full-blown eating disorder.

What are eating disorders?

Most people still believe that teens need to be dangerously underweight to be diagnosed with an eating disorder. But this is a myth: teens at a healthy weight can be diagnosed with eating disorders, too.

Anorexia nervosa and bulimia nervosa may be the most widely recognized eating disorders, but in recent years Other Specified Feeding or Eating Disorder (or OSFED) has been an increasingly common diagnosis. Teens with OSFED have many of the symptoms of anorexia or bulimia but they don't meet full criteria for either disorder, and they may not be underweight. But this fact doesn't make OSFED a less serious eating disorder; like anorexia or bulimia, OSFED is a serious eating disorder that warrants intervention.

Eating disorders: what to look out for

Eating disorders affect more than just weight — they change how someone thinks, feels, and acts around food — and more emphasis needs to be given to these signs and symptoms.

Eating disordered thoughts and feelings

+ A strong desire to lose weight or an intense fear of weight gain.
+ Excessive worry about food and eating.
+ Anxiety around meals, and guilt after eating.
+ Rigid thoughts about food being 'good' or 'bad'.
+ A preoccupation with body shape and weight.
+ Rigid rules for eating (e.g. 'I should only eat when I'm hungry' or 'I shouldn't eat carbohydrates').
+ Extreme body dissatisfaction.

Behavioural signs of an eating disorder

+ Dietary restriction.
+ Avoidance of certain foods or whole groups of food.
+ Complaints about certain foods triggering digestive discomfort (in the absence of a physical cause).
+ An increased interest in food preparation and cooking meals independently.

+ Rigid patterns of eating (e.g. needing to eat meals and snacks at specific times).
+ Signs of agitation when preferred food options aren't available.
+ Eating alone instead of with the rest of the family.
+ Binge eating or evidence of food hoarding.
+ Excessive exercise, including exercising when sick or injured.
+ Frequent use of the bathroom scales.
+ Secretive behaviour around food.

Physical signs of an eating disorder

+ Weight loss or weight fluctuations.
+ More frequent illness (due to a weakened immune system).
+ Light headedness.
+ Tiredness and feelings of lethargy.
+ Disturbed appetite.
+ Concentration problems.
+ Digestive problems (e.g. feeling bloated).

When should I be worried?

Not all teens who diet will develop an eating disorder, but dieting is the most common indicator of the onset of an eating disorder. If your teen does start dieting, be on the lookout for other early warning signs like the ones listed below.

+ Sudden dietary changes (e.g. changing to a vegetarian or vegan diet).
+ An increased interest in 'healthy' eating.
+ Following 'thinspiration' or 'fitspiration' accounts on social media.
+ Eating smaller portions or skipping snacks/meals.
+ Wanting to eat alone, away from the rest of the family.

+ Changes to weight.
+ Agitation and a reluctance to eat at meal times.
+ Low body confidence.
+ Increased use of bathroom scales.
+ The use of calorie counting apps.

If your teen starts to tick multiple boxes, seek professional advice. If, like Alison's parents, you're unsure how concerned you need to be, make an appointment anyway. If it's nothing, having the opinion of a professional will give you peace of mind, but if your teen is starting to show early signs of an eating disorder, early intervention is critical.

Investigate sudden changes to your daughter's diet

Healthy eating might seem healthy, but rigid food rules and weight loss-inspired eating can make teens vulnerable to ongoing issues with both food and body image. If your daughter develops an interest in 'healthy' living, look beyond her food and exercise choices to her motivation. Find out what healthy living means to her, and why eating healthy foods is so important. If her reasons are weight related, encourage a different agenda, but know that you'll need to do more than just tell your daughter she's beautiful the way she is and doesn't need to lose weight. It doesn't matter how genuine you are, you're her parent. By default, she'll assume your compliment is biased and your words will fall on deaf ears.

Explain why diets don't work

Steer your daughter away from weight loss-inspired eating by helping her to see diets as a waste of her time. Start by introducing her to set-point theory. Set-point theory is the theory that the human body has a natural weight range, called your 'set point', that it's genetically predisposed to maintain. When you're in a healthy weight range, your body compensates and adjusts when it needs to, to keep you at your set point. If you sometimes eat a bit more than your body needs, your metabolism automatically speeds up to burn off the extra calories you've consumed. Likewise, if you occasionally eat less than you need, your body adjusts to use fuel more efficiently to circumvent weight loss.

Because your daughter's weight is genetically pre-determined, if she's within a healthy weight range her body will fight to keep her within this range, even if she diets. That said, the body can only compensate for an inadequate fuel supply for so long. There's a chance long-term dieting will result in her losing weight below her set-point, but a growing body of research suggests that teens who diet are actually more likely to *gain* weight over the longer-term than teens who don't. In their 2006 study, for example, Neumark-Sztainer and colleagues found that dieting teens were nearly twice as likely as non-dieting teens to be overweight within five years.[2]

Another interesting study — a large scale twin study by Pietiläinen and colleagues in 2012 — showed that a teen's risk for weight gain increased in line with the number of diets they'd been on; teens with more dieting experience were more at risk for weight gain later in life than teens who'd been on fewer diets. What's more, their results showed that while genes likely influence the effectiveness of diets longer-term, the connection between diets and weight gain can't only be explained by genes. Identical twins who differed with respect to their dieting history — one twin had a history of dieting while the other twin did not — showed different weight patterns. Identical twins with a history of dieting were heavier in early adulthood than their co-twins, suggesting that dieting in and of itself is significantly associated with an increased risk of weight gain, independent of genes.[3]

Encourage a 'food as fuel' food philosophy

You can help your daughter adopt a healthy relationship with food by helping her to focus on what food does for her body. Encourage her to eat protein for growth and repair, complex carbohydrates so her body has the energy it needs to breathe and move, and fats so fat-soluble essential vitamins like vitamins A, D, E, and K can be transported around her body.

When she participates in sport, remind her to eat before playing so she has the energy she needs to play well, and prompt her to re-fuel afterwards so that her body can recover. During exams, suggest she eats complex carbohydrates so her brain has the fuel it needs to concentrate and retain information, and foods high in magnesium — nuts, bananas, leafy greens, and avocados — to help her muscles relax. When she's tired and run down encourage her to eat citrus fruits, strawberries, leafy green vegetables and other high vitamin C foods to boost her immune system, and encourage her to reflect on whether an unbalanced diet might be playing a role in her low energy levels.

Encourage balance and flexibility

You can also build your daughter's resilience against body image and food-related issues by encouraging her to eat a balanced, flexible diet. Recommend that she eat all kinds of foods, even chocolate, sweets, burgers and fries — just encourage her to eat foods like this on a sometimes and not an every-meal basis. When her balance is out and you have to talk to her about her diet, don't use the threat of weight gain to discourage her from eating foods that are high in sugar or saturated fats; offer explanations that focus on fuel quality instead.

Explain that food is just food, it's not good or bad but, like the different fuel options for cars, some foods are a better quality energy source than others. Simple carbohydrates like chocolate, soft drinks/ sodas and biscuits/cookies are simple sugars that the body breaks down relatively easily for a quick, short burst of energy. Complex carbohydrates, on the other hand — found in vegetables, wholegrain cereals, multigrain bread and some rice — are broken down more slowly and offer a longer lasting, better quality source of fuel. Make sure she knows that relying on simple carbohydrates for energy will make her feel heavy, tired and lethargic, but eating complex carbohydrates can help her to feel more positive and energetic.

Avoid food labels

Be mindful of the way you talk about food in front of your daughter and avoid labelling foods as good or bad, even if only in passing. Even comments like, 'I'm trying to be good this week, I really shouldn't' encourage an unhealthy, weight-focused food philosophy and one that detracts from the food-as-fuel approach you're trying to help her adopt.

Encourage alternate motivations for exercise

When it comes to exercise, steer clear of conversations about burning calories. Help your daughter want to exercise to reduce stress, improve mood, strengthen immunity, build strength or achieve fitness goals like participating in a fun run or being able to swim a certain number of laps of the pool — any reason that's meaningful to her and doesn't relate to calories. Tying exercise to calories will keep your daughter stuck in a weight-loss agenda, which will increase the likelihood of her dieting, and also the chance of her falling into the trap of measuring her self-worth via her weight.

Model a healthy relationship with food

What will ultimately determine whether your daughter has a healthy relationship with food is the lessons she learns about food from *you*. Your actions will set a more powerful example than your words, so practise what you preach. Steer away from diets and weight loss-focused food talk and adopt a food-as-fuel food philosophy instead.

Eat a balanced diet and try not to be too restrictive in your approach to healthy eating. Eat all foods, including 'sometimes' foods like chocolate and sweet biscuits/cookies, and try to avoid stocking the fridge and pantry with too many fat-free/sugar-free/gluten-free/low-carb products. It won't affect your weight to eat a piece of chocolate or full-cream yoghurt every now and then, but it will provide the foundation your daughter needs to have a healthy relationship with food.

When moderation goes out the window — which it almost certainly will during holidays and periods of celebration — avoid eating less or exercising more to compensate for this. Not only is compensation ineffective, it also subtly promotes weight-focused eating and exercise. At the end of the day your daughter will follow what you do not what you say, so let your actions be her teacher.

The important bits

+ Teenage diets are often dismissed as a passing phase, but healthy eating isn't always healthy and diets should be given more attention.
+ Diets encourage rigid food rules that can lead to an unbalanced diet and inadequate nutrition.
+ Teens who diet are at higher risk for body image issues.
+ Not all teens who diet will develop an eating disorder, but dieting increases the risk of the onset of an eating disorder.

+ DO help your daughter to understand that diets are ineffective and can actually cause weight gain.
+ DO help your daughter to focus on the function of food for her body.
+ DO help your daughter to find an alternate motivation for exercise (and one that's unrelated to weight loss).
+ DON'T label food as 'good' or 'bad'.
+ DO encourage a balanced, flexible approach to eating.
+ DO be a good role model by adopting a 'food as fuel' food philosophy.

4

WHEN YOUR DAUGHTER'S A DRAMA QUEEN

Teenage girls have a reputation for being dramatic. They can be hypersensitive and quick to blow things out of proportion, not to mention short-tempered and over-emotional. The exaggerated nature of your daughter's emotional meltdowns can make it hard to take her concerns seriously, but adolescence is a stressful and tumultuous time. Throughout her teenage years your daughter will have to cope with everyday stressors like academic pressure, pressure from friends to be popular and thin, and stressful relationships with peers who are just as emotionally reactive as she is. She'll also have to deal with bigger stressors, like finding her place in the world, discovering who she is and figuring out what she wants to do with the rest of her life. When viewed through adult eyes, her stressors may seem trivial, but it's unfair to compare her stressors to yours. Her stress might not come in the form of a hefty mortgage or an overzealous boss, but that doesn't make it any less valid. The stress she feels is just as real as yours, regardless of the cause.

While most teens intuitively develop skills for coping with the stressors they face, some teens struggle. They lack the skills they need to contain their distress, and their emotional meltdowns and explosive outbursts are often symptomatic of a bigger issue: anxiety.

Anxiety: what is it?

Anxiety is a normal emotion. Most people feel at least some degree of anxiety in response to stressful situations, but if your daughter feels anxious or worried on a regular basis, or if her anxiety makes it hard for her to do the things she wants or needs to do, her distress might be more than normal anxiety; it might be symptomatic of an anxiety disorder.

What are anxiety disorders?

There are a number of different anxiety disorders, each with a slightly different set of symptoms. The most common anxiety disorders in teens are listed for you below.

Generalized anxiety disorder: This is an anxiety disorder characterized by persistent and excessive worry about any number of things — for example, worry about academic performance and failure, the health and wellbeing of family and friends, catastrophic events or the future.

Social anxiety: Anxiety that's triggered by social situations and worry about being negatively evaluated and judged by others is known as social anxiety. When it's severe, social anxiety can make it hard for teens to go to school or socialize outside school hours.

Specific phobias: Phobias are an intense fear of specific objects or situations — for example, heights (acrophobia), flying (aviophobia) or enclosed spaces (claustrophobia). When teens have a specific phobia, they usually go out of their way to avoid contact with whatever it is that makes them anxious.

Panic disorder: A panic attack is the sudden occurrence of intense and overwhelming fear and distress — they can be pretty scary. Teens with panic disorder have panic attacks regularly. They worry about what their attacks mean, and when their next panic attack will hit.

Obsessive-compulsive disorder: Teens with obsessive-compulsive disorder experience intrusive and distressing thoughts or images known as obsessions, and they feel the need to perform rituals — also known as compulsions — to manage the anxiety these obsessions trigger. Obsessions and compulsions can be really disruptive to a teen's day-to-day life.

Why do teens develop anxiety?

There's no simple answer for why some teens develop anxiety and others don't, but certain factors do put teens at higher risk. One of the strongest risk factors for anxiety is temperament. Some teens are born with an anxious temperament and are wary of new situations and unfamiliar people right from the start, regardless of their early experiences. Environmental factors can also play a role. Having anxious parents can make teens more vulnerable for anxiety, as can stressful life events like family conflict, relationship break-ups or school stress.

That said, the relationship between risk factors and anxiety is complex and not all 'at-risk' teens will develop anxiety. A teen's risk can be counterbalanced by their exposure to protective factors, like the development of skills for challenging anxious thoughts, or parents who discourage avoidance of anxiety-provoking situations. Importantly, the influence of protective factors means that even anxiety-prone teens can avoid anxiety disorders if they grow up in the right environment.

Is anxiety really all that common in teens?

It's easy to mistake emotional outbursts for teenage drama, but it's important to make sure your daughter's meltdowns aren't a sign of something more. A 2015 survey examining the mental health of Australian children and adolescents found that nearly 8 per cent of all teenage girls aged twelve to seventeen years are living with anxiety.[1] Worldwide data is even more alarming. According to research cited by the National Institute of Mental Health, a whopping 30 per cent of teenage girls in the United States are affected by anxiety.[2] *Thirty per cent.* And that doesn't take into account teens suffering from anxiety worse than what would be considered 'normal' but less severe than what meets the criteria for an anxiety disorder, or teens suffering from anxiety that's still undiagnosed. It's a significant figure and, perhaps unsurprisingly, it makes anxiety the most common mental health disorder affecting teenage girls today.

How do I know if my daughter is anxious?

Anxious teens will have some symptoms in common, but their symptoms will also differ depending on the type of their anxiety. Take Isobel and

Clare, for example. Isobel is in Year 10 and her parents are worried about the amount of pressure she puts on herself to do well at school.

> Isobel's a bit of a perfectionist — she takes after her dad in that way. She's very organized. Her room is always spotless and she's always been a diligent student, right from day dot. We joke about her being the only student who's ever actually liked doing homework.
>
> Up till now, she's never caused us any real problems — it's her sister who's always kept us on our toes — but she's been on edge lately, and last week she came home in tears, really upset about her exam results. We thought she'd done really well — all of her marks were great — but she was really upset. She puts so much pressure on herself, even her teachers have commented on it, but it doesn't seem to matter what anyone says; to her, nothing's ever good enough.
>
> She was so stressed in the lead-up to her exams. She wasn't eating properly or sleeping well at all. All she did was study, and she was in tears over one thing or another nearly every day. And she's only in Year 10! She's got two more years until her final high school exams!
>
> There were so many nights when I tried to get her to close her books and go to bed, but she wouldn't. The more I pushed, the more hysterical she got and it just seemed to make everything worse. She's bitten my head off more times than I can count in the last few weeks. Her behaviour's been appalling, which is really not like

her. I know it's just stress so we leave her be, but I'm still really worried about how late she's staying up studying.

We've tried to help her as much as we can. We've told her she doesn't have to do her usual chores around the house, and I've been driving her to school each day so she doesn't have to get the bus — she's just so tired in the mornings, so at least if I drive her she gets a bit of extra sleep. I even proofread her assignments for her (she gets nervous about missing mistakes) but none of what we do seems to really make a difference.

There are times when she seems relaxed and happy, and I think we're out of the woods, but then something happens — usually something to do with her workload at school, or sometimes it's issues with her friends — and she gets stressed and upset again. Things seem to be getting worse rather than better, and we don't know how to help.

While Isobel's anxiety is largely about school, Clare on the other hand feels anxious in social situations.

Clare's always been our sensitive child. She worries too much about what people think and puts a lot of effort into making other people happy. She's a bit of a people pleaser really, and has been since she was little.

Clare's just never seemed as resilient as our other two kids. She's always been shy and hates being around big groups of people. She has a small group of friends at school, but she doesn't spend much time with them outside school hours, and she's not involved in any of the activities other kids do after school. We used to think she was just a bit of a homebody, so we didn't push her to get involved, but now we're starting to wonder whether it's more than that.

She seems really anxious in social situations, even amongst groups of people she knows. Last week's a good example. It was her best friend's birthday party and she really wanted to go, but there was a large group of people going — her friend Caitlin is a bit of a social butterfly — and she was anxious and stressed about it all week. She doesn't usually talk to us about how she's feeling, but she broke down one night and actually opened up. She was stressed that she wouldn't know what to say to the other kids, and that everyone else would have someone to talk to and she'd be left out. She's convinced the other kids think she's boring and only put up with her at school because she's friends with Caitlin. I try to tell her that that's not true — she gets asked to things all the time, she just never goes — but she wouldn't have a bar of it, and the more I tried to talk to her, the more upset she got.

The thing is (and I know we're probably biased), Clare's actually a really likeable kid. She's kind and caring, and funny, and I think the other kids do actually like her — she just needs to come out of her shell a little. We're starting to wonder whether letting her keep to herself has been the right thing to do. I just wish she had more confidence.

Common symptoms of anxiety in teens

Symptoms of anxiety commonly seen in teens are things like:

+ blowing things out of proportion and worrying more than necessary
+ wanting to avoid situations, people or objects that cause anxiety
+ feeling upset and distressed in anticipation of anxiety-provoking situations
+ feeling tight, tense and on edge
+ physical symptoms of anxiety (e.g. nausea, headaches, a racing heart)
+ irritability or agitation
+ anxiety about new or unfamiliar situations
+ trouble sleeping
+ changes to appetite
+ problems with concentration.

Other signs of anxiety in teens can be:

+ worrying too much about what other people think
+ worrying about everyday situations (e.g. problems with friends) more than other teens do
+ worrying about bad things happening
+ problems switching off from worries
+ being sensitive to criticism
+ feeling self-conscious and uncomfortable around other people
+ chronic procrastination
+ feeling easily overwhelmed and stressed
+ problems making decisions
+ seeking reassurance from others about doing tasks correctly or the 'right way'

+ not being able to relax
+ exhibiting challenging behaviour, such as talking back during stressful periods.

If your daughter does show signs and symptoms of anxiety, don't panic. Not all teens who are anxious will struggle with anxiety in adulthood, and catching your daughter's anxiety now is a good thing. Early identification means she has the opportunity to learn how to manage and challenge her anxious symptoms from the outset, and this may well be what ends up helping her to avoid anxiety later in life.

Help her dial down her anxious thoughts

When your daughter's anxious, her head will be drawn to worst-case scenarios, and small things — even things that aren't worth worrying about — will trigger huge, over-the-top reactions. Her overly dramatic, frantic meltdowns might make you want to scream, but as frustrating as they are, they're not entirely her fault. Anxiety is a powerful emotion and it can affect not just how your daughter feels, but what she thinks as well. It makes worst-case scenarios seem more likely than they are and it will trick her into thinking she can't cope, even if she can. Once anxiety takes hold, your daughter will have a hard time thinking clearly and she'll need your help to get her thinking back on track — but there are a few things you need to keep in mind if you're going to be effective in your approach.

Trying to have a logical conversation with your daughter when she's in the midst of a meltdown won't work. Her anxiety will make it hard for her to take in much of what you say, and when she senses your frustration it'll only make things worse. What your daughter needs in moments of panic is a calm, soothing voice. Reassure her that you're there, remind her that her anxiety will pass, and help her to feel safe.

That's not to say that you can't help your daughter challenge her anxiety, because you can; but when it comes to anxiety, timing is everything. Wait until her anxiety has lessened, or if you know what her triggers are, get in well ahead of time and start the conversation early. Encourage her to talk to you about her fears, and when she does, listen but don't talk. And avoid comments like 'well that's just silly' or 'you don't need to worry about that' because they won't help your daughter any. Worse, they'll make her feel embarrassed and misunderstood, and you can bet it'll be the first and last time she talks to you about how she's feeling.

If your daughter seems relatively calm, try to help her keep her worries in perspective. Don't tell her what to think; instead, ask questions that will help her consider a different point of view. The exact questions you ask will depend a little on her area of worry, but questions like the ones below are good examples.

+ Have you worried about this before?
+ What happened last time you worried about this?
+ Did what you were worried about come true or was your anxiety misleading?
+ Putting aside what your anxiety's telling you for a minute, based on past experience, what do you think the *actual* likelihood is of this worst-case scenario happening?
+ Is there anything we can do about this situation?
+ What parts of the situation do you have control over?

Challenging anxious thoughts is a difficult skill and it's one your daughter will need to practise, but over time it will become a tool she can use to better manage her anxiety. Help her to practise, but time your practice well, and be patient. The more frustrated you get, the more anxious she'll feel, and things will end badly. Stay calm enough for the both of you and she'll get there in the end.

Parenting an anxious teen 101: avoid avoidance

How you respond to your daughter when she's anxious is important. She'll want to avoid any situation — a class speech, a difficult assignment, social situations — that makes her feel anxious, and in fact the more anxious she is the more she'll want to avoid. Your love for her will compel you to do whatever you can to protect her from feeling stressed, but while helping her to avoid stress might seem like a good solution, the reality is, going along with her anxiety and encouraging avoidance will actually make her anxiety worse.

When your daughter sidesteps anxiety-provoking situations she'll initially feel relief, but it's only a short-term solution for her distress. Avoidance prevents her from learning that worst-case scenarios aren't nearly as likely as her anxiety would have her believe, and this can make her anxiety worse in the long term. Over time, avoidance can also undermine her confidence. It cheats her of the opportunity to see that she can cope with far more than she gives herself credit for, opening the door for anxiety to start infiltrating other areas of her life as well.

Think back to Clare on p. 45. Her parents have always supported her preference to avoid spending time with friends outside school hours, but this hasn't really helped to solve her problem. Avoidance may have helped Clare to feel less stressed in the short-term, but longer-term it's affected her confidence and it's made her anxiety worse overall. After years of avoidance, Clare's anxiety is so bad she's convinced no one likes her and she panics at the thought of spending time with people in social contexts, even people she knows quite well.

Clare's parents thought they were doing the right thing. They wanted Clare to be happy and thought they were being helpful, but unfortunately they've inadvertently fallen into the trap of helping to make her anxiety worse. Had they encouraged Clare to face her fears from a younger age, things might be different for her now, but all's not lost. It's never too late to turn things around.

Facing anxiety head-on

To beat her anxiety, your daughter will need to confront, not avoid, the things that make her anxious. Unfortunately, this also means she's going to have to feel worse before she feels better and *you'll* have to withstand the meltdowns this will inevitably trigger.

Feeling more anxious in order to feel less anxious might seem backwards, but not all anxiety is the same: there's a difference between wasteful and productive anxiety. Wasteful anxiety is the anxiety your teen is living with right now; it's relentless and exhausting, and it serves no real purpose other than to make her feel bad. Productive anxiety feels just as awful, but it serves a purpose: it's anxiety your daughter is intentionally experiencing as a step towards feeling less anxious in the future.

Confronting anxiety works because when your daughter faces her fears, she's blessed with the benefit of hindsight. She gets to see that after all her worry, her worst fears didn't come true, or if they did, that the outcome wasn't nearly as bad as she thought it would be. She learns through direct experience — which is always more powerful than learning through lectures — that her anxiety is misleading: not only does it trick her into thinking that worst-case scenarios are more likely than they actually are, it makes her underestimate how capable she is.

51

Facing anxiety head-on will initially make your daughter more anxious, but the anxiety she experiences will be productive. By facing her fears she'll accumulate knowledge she can use to question the validity of her worries, and while it's harder for her in the short-term, it's what will ultimately help her to regain control over her anxiety.

Convincing your teen to face her anxiety

Encouraging your daughter to confront her anxiety is the key to helping her to feel less anxious, but it's easier said than done. The idea of facing her fears will be less than appealing to your teen, and she'll probably hate the idea. If the choice is between feeling sick to her stomach and suffering through intense anxiety versus not, she'll choose not to — and to be fair, so probably would you. Intellectually, she might understand how confronting her anxiety will help her to feel less anxious in the future, but knowing this won't necessarily be enough to inspire her to face her fears in the present. For her to even consider the idea, you'll need to give her a reason to pause and take stock — and that's where rewards come in.

When it comes to convincing teens to face their anxiety, rewards are a powerful tool. When used correctly, rewards can help teens to tolerate their anxiety long enough to successfully face their fears, but there are a couple of things you need to keep in mind. First, rewards only work if they're meaningful, so when it comes to setting specific rewards, get your daughter's input — don't assume you know what she wants. Second, with anxiety, the trick is using rewards that are big enough to counterbalance your daughter's urge to avoid. So before you say no to her suggestions, think about how big of an issue her anxiety is and be guided by that. For smaller issues, smaller rewards will do, but if her anxiety is at the more severe end of the spectrum, you might need to bring out the big guns. And if you're worried offering incentives will make your daughter dependent on rewards to cope — don't be. With practice, her confidence will grow, her anxiety will lessen and you won't need rewards to spur her into action. Rest assured, rewards will help to get things moving in the right direction, but they won't need to be part of your longer-term strategy.

When rewards don't work

If your teen isn't motivated by rewards, no matter how enticing, you may need to change your approach to include consequences. As harsh as it probably sounds, if anxiety is interfering with your teen's life and incentives aren't helping to boost her motivation, you'll need to add something to the mix to help her to pause and reflect on the longer-term impact of her choices. Her anxiety will make her short-sighted: it will make her want to do whatever she can to not feel anxious in the here and now, but this instinct will keep her stuck. A meaningful consequence can motivate your teen to think twice and, if used correctly, can help her to choose a more helpful course of action.

Consequences work like this. Say your teen is refusing to go to school because she's anxious about a speech she has to give in English. You've tried reassuring her and telling her that it doesn't matter if she makes a mistake, but she's not giving an inch and you can't physically drag her to school. You feel bad for your teen but you're also frustrated because you've offered to help her practise public speaking numerous times in the last few weeks, and she's declined your offers of help each and every time.

You may not be able to force your teen to go to school, but you can offer her a forced choice. You can gently tell her that you're sorry she's feeling so anxious and you're happy to help her in any way you can, but you unfortunately can't condone her not going to school because you refuse to let her anxiety win. Offer to help drive her to school or to speak to her teachers for extra support, but explain that if she chooses to stay home, you won't be able to write her a note excusing her from school, and she'll have to face detention for skipping class without parent consent.

When your daughter reacts badly to your forced choice — as she probably will — tell her that you know it must feel as if she's being punished for feeling anxious, and you're sorry that it feels that way, but you're not trying to punish her, you're trying to support her making decisions that will help her to master her anxiety. Her anxiety will make it hard for her to see your point of view, but don't get drawn into an argument. Empathize with how she's feeling but stick to your plan. Seeing your daughter distressed will be hard, but watching her struggle with anxiety for the rest of her life will be harder. When you feel yourself relenting, remember that your daughter will continue to feel anxious regardless of whether or not you intervene, but the anxiety she suffers through will be wasteful anxiety. When you help your daughter to confront the situations she'd rather avoid she experiences productive anxiety, and it's productive anxiety that will ultimately help her to feel less anxious longer-term.

If your daughter chooses to confront her anxiety, give her lots of praise and make sure she knows how proud you are of her for facing her fears. If she chooses to avoid the situation that's making her anxious, that's her choice, but make sure you follow through with the consequences you discussed. Consequences might not have been enough to inspire her to face her fears this time, but knowing you're serious about following through with the consequences you set might help her to make a different decision next time.

And if rewards and consequences both don't work, then what?

If you continue to have a hard time convincing your daughter to face her fears despite meaningful rewards and consequences, her anxiety might be at the higher end of the spectrum and she may need a more graduated approach to reducing avoidance.

If she's anxious about giving speeches, for example, when it comes to school assessments she might cope better if she's offered the option of delivering her speech to a smaller group of peers she feels more comfortable with — as opposed to the class as a whole — just until she gains more confidence. If attending parties is the issue, she might not be able to attend large parties at first, but she might be able to tolerate smaller parties for a shorter period of time.

Taking smaller steps will make it a slower process, but if her anxiety is more severe, you'll see faster progress overall with a slow and steady approach.

When anxiety turns into challenging behaviour

It's hard to watch your teen struggle with anxiety, but your empathy tank can start to run low when her anxiety is expressed through tantrums, irritability and general surliness. It's easy to forget that anxiety is the real culprit, and her meltdowns and uncharacteristic rudeness can push your buttons and make you react angrily out of frustration. Alternatively, you might be all too aware that anxiety is behind your teen's short fuse, and be more willing to excuse her poor behaviour as a result — like Isobel's parents earlier in this chapter

— but this isn't necessarily a better approach. Your intention may be to help ease her stress, but changing the rules to accommodate her anxiety can backfire.

Consistent boundaries make an environment predictable and it's this predictability that helps anxious teens to feel safe. Abandoning your usual rules and tiptoeing around your daughter's anxiety might help her to avoid upset in the present, but this relief will be short-lived and longer-term your actions will make her feel vulnerable and out of control. Coming down hard on her and reacting angrily isn't helpful, either. Not only will it contribute to your daughter feeling misunderstood, there's also the possibility that it will make her anxiety worse.

It's important to stick to the same rules you've always had, even when your teen is having a hard time. What you *can* change, though, is the way you enforce these boundaries: you can enforce them with more compassion. Consider this scenario. You ask your teen a question about an assignment you know is due next week, and she responds (because she's anxious about the assignment) by screaming at you to leave her alone. It's not the first time she's lost her temper this week and you've had enough. You yell back, lecture her about her attitude, and ground her for the next month, at which point she storms off to her room to stew over the injustice of her punishment.

Screaming at you is unacceptable, period. Your daughter needs to be held accountable for her behaviour, but she's also not completely herself at the moment because she's struggling with anxiety. Her anxiety doesn't excuse her behaviour, and it doesn't mean she should be given a free pass, but it is something you need to keep in mind when you enforce consequences.

A compassionate boundary

A compassionate boundary balances acknowledgment of anxiety with the need for accountability. Using the example above, a compassionate boundary might look like this:

Parent: (*after giving teen 15–20 minutes to cool off*) I want to talk to you about what just happened. It sounds like you're having a hard time at the moment and I'm sorry you're feeling so bad. Is there anything you want to talk to me about?

Teen: I'm just really stressed about this assignment. It's really hard and it's taking longer than I thought to get it done. I have a test I need to study for next week as well and I don't know how I'm going to get everything done.

Parent: (*knowing that what teen needs when she's upset is empathy and a listening ear, not advice or reprimands*) I know you've had a lot on your plate recently and it's a busy time at school.

Teen: And I have work tomorrow as well, and Amanda's party tomorrow night. I don't know how I'm supposed to fit everything in.

Parent: (*seeing an opportunity to be empathic*) It's really hard to juggle everything when there's so much on. I can understand now why you got so upset earlier. You were trying to have a break and not think about things for a while and I interrupted that when I asked about your assignment. Is there anything I can do to help?

Teen: No, not really, I just need to do work this afternoon.

Parent: (*knowing that a boundary needs to be set*) Okay, well if you change your mind or if you think of something I can do to help, just let me know, I'm happy to do what I can to help you. And I am really sorry that you're feeling so stressed, but I do need you to try to not bite my head off even if I do ask a question at the wrong time. It's okay to let me know you're stressed and you don't want to talk about it then and there, but it's not okay to yell at me like that.

Teen: (*silence*)

Parent: I'm not going to ground you for a month. I said that in frustration, but I am going to ask you to hand me your phone for 24 hours to help you remember to make a different choice next time. I'll leave you to it now so you can get on with your work, but if you need anything, just let me know.

In the example above, you've still sent a clear message that your daughter's earlier behaviour is unacceptable and she'll be held accountable accordingly, but the consequence you've enforced is fairer and your compassionate approach shows her that while you understand and are willing to help, you won't tolerate rudeness.

In the heat of the moment it can be hard to know what to do. Part of you will feel compelled to enforce harsher consequences than usual because your daughter's anxiety-fuelled behaviour is so infuriating, and the other part of you may be tempted to be more lenient because her behaviour is out of character and so clearly the result of her current distress. If you're ever in doubt about how to manage challenging behaviour in your anxious teen, ask yourself what you'd do if she wasn't anxious and then do that, but with compassion. Your teen may be having a hard time, but she still needs boundaries.

The important bits

+ Whether or not a teen develops anxiety depends on the balance of their exposure to risk factors and protective factors.
+ Symptoms of anxiety can vary between teens and can be physical, emotional and behavioural.
+ Anxiety will make your daughter want to avoid the situations, people and places that trigger her anxiety.
+ Avoidance will help your daughter to feel less stressed in the short-term, but it will make her more anxious longer-term.
+ You can help your daughter overcome her anxiety by helping her to face her fears.
+ Confronting her anxiety will make your daughter more anxious in the short-term, but less anxious longer-term.
+ Rewards and consequences can help motivate your teen to confront her anxiety.
+ Anxiety can cause teens to be irritable and agitated, and to behave in a way that's out of character.
+ A compassionate approach to boundary setting will help you to foster the right balance between holding your anxious teen accountable for unreasonable behaviour and validating her distress.

5

WHEN YOUR DAUGHTER WON'T GET OFF HER PHONE

Over the course of her teenage years, your daughter will spend an astonishing amount of time attached to her smartphone. With so many apps at her fingertips — Facebook, Instagram, Snapchat and WhatsApp, just to name a few — chances are her phone will get more attention than her homework, and she'll spend more time engaged in electronic exchanges with friends than face-to-face interactions with family. As a parent, you'll think her phone use is excessive and unreasonable, and you'll struggle to understand why she finds it so challenging to tear her eyes away from a pocket-sized screen long enough to have a conversation with the people around her. Her phone-induced deafness will test your patience, as will the 50 or so texts she sends each day, and the excess usage charges that sneak their way onto your phone bill each month despite the numerous conversations you've had with her about her data limit.

It's healthy and normal for your teen to want to use her phone to connect with friends, but she also needs to learn to balance her need to connect with digital-free downtime. You can force her to correct her balance by taking away her phone, but it's a short-term fix and one that won't help her learn the skills she needs to moderate her own phone use longer-term.

What your teen really needs is help to learn the skills she needs to self-monitor. Teaching skills for self-monitoring is more work up-front, but it's also a more permanent solution.

Managing your daughter's phone usage

I've lost count of the number of times phone use has come up as an issue in my sessions. If there's a teen in the vicinity, phone use seems to be an issue. 'She's on her phone *all* the time, it's infuriating!' is a phrase I hear most days. 'Nothing we've tried works!' is another. And when it comes to discouraging excessive phone usage, nine times out of ten the issue is this: parents are trying to convince their teens to spend less time on their phones by presenting them with information about the harmful effects of too much screen time. For the record, it never works. *You* might be concerned about the impact of phone use on your daughter's sleep and concentration, but she couldn't care less. Her phone makes her happy in the here and now and that's all she really cares about. That she'll be tired tomorrow or that her productivity might be affected isn't cause for concern — missing out on a group chat though, that would be a crisis, so putting down her phone is out of the question.

Debating your daughter's phone use will get you nowhere fast. You'll never be able to make sense of her need to be constantly connected, and she'll never understand why you're so uptight about her being on her phone, when — from her point of view — you're on your phone nearly as much as she is. Just a quick side note on this, because it's an issue that comes up a lot. When you lecture your teen about her phone use, be prepared for the fact that you're leaving yourself wide open to questions from her about *your* phone usage. If you regularly answer calls, respond to texts or check emails on your phone at home, she may query why it's okay for you to check your phone so frequently when it's not okay for her. Think before you react to this. You'll feel compelled to argue that your phone use is irrelevant and none of her business, or to differentiate your phone use from hers on the basis that your usage is work related, but neither argument will get you very far. Double standards will always be a sore point with your teen, and your insinuation that her phone use is unimportant will only add more fuel to the fire. It might not be your usual approach, but acknowledging your daughter's feedback and admitting you need to have better boundaries with your phone too will be a more effective strategy.

Admitting your faults might feel uncomfortable, but it'll help you to be effective. If you persist with your double standards, you'll lose her respect and end up on opposite sides of the problem. Think about how you'd feel if your boss continually gave you a hard time about not putting in enough hours, but left at 4.30 pm each day to play golf. How much respect would you have for him and how willing would you be to comply with his requests? Don't be afraid to acknowledge when your teen is right; she'll respect you for it.

When it comes to your daughter's phone use, the two of you will never see eye to eye. You can persist with longwinded lectures and present her with information about the dangers of overuse, but neither strategy will get you very far. As backwards as it sounds, the best thing you can do is agree to disagree. Accept that her phone is important to her for reasons you'll never understand, and instead of setting rigid rules that discount this, work *with* her to reach a mutually agreeable solution. Negotiating with your teen might feel uncomfortable at first, especially if you're used to ruling with an iron fist, but don't let that get in the way of you giving it a go. If you want your daughter to be more flexible and less argumentative, you're going to need to lead by example, and negotiation is the key to getting things back on track. In her teenage years, negotiation will be one of the most powerful parenting strategies you have at your disposal – use it.

Negotiate reasonable limits

When your daughter tells you she *needs* her phone, resist the urge to roll your eyes, and try to see things from her point of view. Take the time to hear her out and don't automatically shoot her down just because her thoughts and opinions are different from your own. Once you've listened, reassure her that you understand that her friends are important to her — it's why you're not looking to ban her from her phone all together — but let her know that you need to find a solution for her phone use that works for both of you, not just her.

Explain your reasons for wanting to work on phone boundaries, but keep it brief. If you deliver a lengthy lecture, your daughter will tune out partway through and your message will get lost. Skipping over your concerns will be just as problematic: your daughter will think you're making rules just to assert your parental control — one of her biggest pet peeves — and she'll be less likely to listen to what you have to say as a result. Be specific and explain what changes you think are needed and why. When she defends her phone use — which she will — don't get drawn into an argument. Reiterate that you're not angling to take her phone away from her, you're starting a conversation about phone boundaries so you can help her to have clearer boundaries between times when she uses her phone and times when she doesn't.

Once you've both had a say, see if you can negotiate a mutually agreeable solution. If her suggestions are a little lax and for more time than you think is reasonable, explain your concerns and put forward an alternate compromise. If in turn she thinks your suggestions are far too strict, listen to what she has to say and, where you can, put forward a modified solution that's in line with her feedback.

Collaborating with your teen on limit-setting will feel strange initially, but commanding compliance will be no more effective with your teen than in any other personal or professional relationship. When you're inflexible, your teen will mirror your inflexibility and your chance at a productive conversation will be lost. You might be sceptical about her ability to suggest acceptable limits, but given the opportunity, she may surprise you with her reasonableness. Give her a chance to prove you wrong and see where it gets you.

The dos and don'ts of effective negotiation

How effective you are in getting your teen to ditch her screen will depend on your approach. Collaborating with her on limit setting might feel backwards, but it will get you so much further than an authoritarian approach. Compare the two conversations below.

Collaborative parenting

Parent: (*gives a neutral explanation of their concern about teen's phone use*) I want to talk to you about how tired you've been lately. I'm concerned you're going to bed later than you should because your school work is taking longer than it used to, and

I think this might have something to do with the fact that your phone is active on your desk while you're working.

Teen: It's really not that big a deal, I've just had heaps of homework lately. I don't know why you always have to blame my phone for everything.

Parent: (*remembering the end goal, avoids getting drawn into an argument over teen's excessive phone use and instead acknowledges teen's point of view*) I know you've been busy at school and I can see how hard you're working; I'd still like us to look at how you can get to bed earlier, though. You might be right, it might not be your phone, but I think having separate times for homework and socializing might be worth a try. How much time do you think is reasonable to set aside for your phone each afternoon?

Teen: Well, I don't always get time to catch up with people properly at school, so I like chatting after school.

Parent: (*sees an opportunity to show teen understanding, then repeats the initial question to kickstart negotiations*) I can understand that, I know some of your friends are in a different class, which makes catching up hard as well. How much time do you need to set aside for catching up?

Teen: I guess a couple of hours?

Parent: (*avoids an exasperated 'seriously?!?' Calmly explains concerns in a neutral way and suggests a more reasonable compromise*) I'm just wondering whether that will work time-wise? By the time you get home from school, finish your homework, and have dinner, if you're on your phone for a couple of hours after that, you'll still be getting to bed quite late. How about if we said half an hour each afternoon after homework?

Teen: Half an hour?!? I may as well not be on my phone at all!

65

Parent: (*resists the urge to argue and encourages teen to suggest an alternate compromise*) Okay, this needs to be a solution that works for both of us, so what might be a better compromise?

Teen: Maybe 45 minutes or an hour?

Parent: (*isn't completely happy with the idea of teen being on her phone for an hour, but chooses to prioritize flexibility and effectiveness over having the last say*) That could work. Maybe you could put your phone on charge when you get home from school while you do your homework, eat, and then you can catch up with friends after that for 45 minutes or so, depending on how much time you have between then and needing to be in bed.

Teen: Okay, I can try that.

'Because I said so' parenting

Parent: You're on your phone way too much and it's got to change. You're tired and grumpy all the time and I'm sick of it. From now on your phone's going on the charger when you get home from school and you're not having it back until your homework's done and we're done with dinner.

Teen: (*feels instantly annoyed by parent's inflexibility and argues back*) But sometimes we don't get home until dinner time — what if I have heaps of homework?

Parent: Then you don't get your phone. Simple. Speak to your friends at school. You don't need to be on your phone nearly as much as you are.

Teen: (*thinks parent's being unreasonable and feels the need to defend herself*) But I don't always get time to catch up with friends at school …

Parent: (*interrupts*) You're there all day, so I find that hard to believe.

I'm done talking about this. It's not up for discussion. No more phone after school.

Teen: *(feels irritated and annoyed and storms off in a huff — taking her phone with her — and silently vows to make her parent's life as difficult as possible for the foreseeable future)*

Negotiating phone limits

The phone limits you negotiate with your teen will differ depending on her age and her specific problem areas, but a few examples are listed for you below. Remember: collaborating with your teen is key, so avoid starting a conversation about phone limits with rigid rules already cemented in your mind.

+ I agree to hand in my phone between the hours of 9.30 pm and 7.30 am.
+ I agree to only use my phone between 7 pm and 7.45 pm after homework is done.
+ I agree to put my phone on airplane mode during homework time.
+ I agree to have 45 minutes of phone-free time each afternoon.
+ I agree to put my phone down when family members are talking to me.
+ I agree and acknowledge that if I'm not able to stick to these limits, my parents will need to add further restrictions to help me have better phone boundaries.

Your daughter won't like handing in her phone because she'll worry about you reading her private messages. Avoid the blow-ups this can cause by letting her add a passcode to her phone before handing it in.

67

Put your plan into action

Once you've established mutually agreeable phone limits, decide how you'll measure progress, then set a time —— ideally within a fortnight of your initial conversation — to discuss how well the new boundaries have worked. Flag for your teen ahead of time that if she's able to stick to the new limits, you'll be happy for her to continue to manage her own phone usage, but if she has difficulty, the two of you may need to review and revise her phone boundaries to help her find the right balance.

Over the course of the trial period, if you notice your teen breaching your agreement, say nothing. Make a note to raise it with her at your meeting, but don't nag. Nagging is part of your old parenting plan and it won't help you to be effective. Your teen craves your trust and respect and she desperately wants more freedom. When you nag her, she feels the need to defend her autonomy, and this will be a barrier to the two of you working effectively together on a solution for her excessive phone use. If you stick to your agreed trial period, she'll appreciate you giving her the opportunity to prove her readiness for more responsibility, and because you've respected her enough to give her a chance, she'll be more willing to accept a review of her phone boundaries in the event that she falls short.

Phone monitoring apps

If you're sceptical about your teen's ability to accurately monitor her phone use over your agreed trial period, phone monitoring apps are a good way to ensure a more objective measure of usage. Two good examples are listed for you below, but there are a number of monitoring apps, each with a slightly different focus. It's worth doing some research to find the app that's right for you.

Moment: screen time tracker: If your daughter has an iPhone, Moment is an app she can use to track how much time she spends on her phone each day and how much time she spends on individual apps such as Facebook or Instagram. As an added benefit, she can use this app to set reminders and daily limits for phone usage too.

AntiSocial: AntiSocial is an app for Android devices that keeps track of a user's daily phone habits. Your daughter can use this app to keep track of her phone use and the time she spends on individual apps, and she can compare her own usage to that of other users as well. If she needs extra help to build healthier phone habits, she can use AntiSocial to block certain apps and restrict her usage too.

Remember to follow through

At the end of your trial period sit down with your teen and ask her how she feels she went with sticking to the limits you agreed on. Don't jump in too soon with your own thoughts and opinions; give her the opportunity to identify what she thinks she did well, and where she thinks she could improve further. If she's mostly stuck to your agreement, give her lots of praise and reinforce that when she's able to have boundaries with her phone, it's a reminder to you that you don't need to micro-manage her as much as you used to. Framing it in this way and linking her success with limit-setting to increased freedom will help her want to continue to maintain good phone boundaries.

In recognition of her efforts, if there's room for you to give your daughter more responsibility (for example, allowing her to keep her phone in her room (switched off) at night rather than her having to hand it in), consider doing this. Not only will this help her practise the skills she needs to independently manage her phone boundaries, it will also reinforce her commitment to making good decisions about her phone use.

When things don't go to plan

If your daughter owns up to not sticking to her limits, or if she's over-generous with her self-assessment and thinks she's done well when she hasn't, don't get drawn into an argument over her lack of success. Arguing about the degree to which she's failed will set you on opposite sides of the problem and prevent you from having a productive conversation. Sidestep this potential pitfall by not engaging in a discussion about who's right and wrong; instead, focus on how you can work together to be more successful in the future.

What your teen needs to do to be more on top of her phone usage might be obvious to you, but avoid being too directive in your approach and give your daughter the opportunity to generate her own solutions for what she'll do differently next time. If you're too demanding, your teen will withdraw from the conversation and this will limit how effective you can be. If you take a more collaborative approach, your daughter will feel respected and this will increase the likelihood of her being an active participant in your discussions.

When given a chance, your daughter might surprise you with her ingenuity. If she doesn't, and you think the ideas she comes up with won't work, consider trialling her solutions anyway for the purpose of proving you're open to taking her ideas seriously. It might mean a longer wait for a solution, but your willingness to take her ideas on board will earn you her respect, and her respect for you is what will ultimately help you to work together to resolve disagreements more effectively.

The important bits

+ Your daughter's phone is an important part of her social world in a way that your phone likely isn't for you.
+ A 'because I said so' approach to parenting, which you might have used in the past, isn't likely to be effective in helping you to change your daughter's phone usage, and persisting with this approach could also drive a wedge between you.
+ DO set limits for her phone use, but change your process.
+ DON'T dictate phone rules.
+ DO negotiate and come to mutually agreeable limits for her phone use.
+ Negotiation will increase the likelihood of your daughter sticking to your agreement, and because it shows her you respect her and are willing to listen to her concerns, odds are it will improve the quality of your relationship as well.

6

WHEN YOUR DAUGHTER STARTS GOING TO PARTIES

When your daughter starts high school, parties will become a regular part of her social calendar. She may have attended parties in primary school, but the parties she wants to attend now will be different. They'll be bigger — anywhere from 40 to 100 people — at the homes of families you've never met, and boys will be part of the mix. The biggest difference, though, is probably this: unlike in primary school, when she attends parties in high school, there's a fair chance she'll be exposed to alcohol and possibly even drugs.

Thinking about your daughter being exposed to drugs and alcohol will make you feel anxious. Your head will jump to all the worst-case scenarios: you'll worry about her safety, her ability to say no if and when she needs to, and the fact that you won't be there to ensure she makes good decisions. Your fear will make you want to ban parties indefinitely, but as tempting as this is, it isn't the best course of action. Saying no to parties will shield your daughter from possible exposure to drugs and alcohol, but it's only a temporary solution. Whether she attends parties or not, she'll be exposed to drugs and alcohol throughout her teenage years, and her young adult years as well.

Not attending parties can also have social consequences for your daughter. Parties are an avenue for her to connect with peers, to have time out from school stress and to practise being independent — if only for a few hours. They provide an opportunity for her to meet new people and widen her circle of friends, and in much the same way that after-work get-togethers can turn professional contacts into personal relationships, spending time with friends at parties can strengthen her existing relationships as well. Yes, she can strengthen her friendships by spending extra time with friends away from the party circuit, but if her friends are attending parties she isn't, it will set her apart from them. Her friends will talk endlessly about the parties they're looking forward to or parties they've been to recently, and because she won't be able to contribute to these conversations, she'll feel excluded and on the outer.

Banning your daughter from parties will be effective insofar as it helps to limit her exposure to drugs and alcohol, but it will impact her relationships, and it won't help her learn the skills she'll one day need to say no. Giving her permission to attend parties without setting limits is also problematic. Unlimited freedom will meet her social needs, but too much freedom too soon can be a catalyst for poor decision-making. As your daughter grows into her independence, what she needs from you is scaffolding: new rules and boundaries that offer her more freedom, and at the same time give her the support she needs to make good decisions.

Not all teens experiment with drugs and alcohol

Taking a step back and giving your teen more freedom might make you nervous, but teens are generally more responsible than we give them credit for. The media gives the impression that teens are wild, irresponsible and out of control, but research tells us that the overwhelming majority of teens *don't* experiment with drugs. The table on p. 76 summarizes the results of four studies that explored drug and alcohol use in teens in Australia, the United States and England. What these studies show is that young people are experimenting with drugs and alcohol later in their teenage years, and a large majority are also choosing to abstain from drugs and alcohol completely. Fewer teens are taking up smoking, and cannabis use (cannabis being the most commonly used drug in teens) has also steadily dropped in the last decade. In fact, cigarette smoking, alcohol consumption and drug use in general have all pretty much declined in the last decade, right across the globe.

The research tells us that most teens are making sensible decisions when it comes to drug and alcohol use. Drugs and alcohol are still cause for concern, and your daughter still needs your help to set limits, but take comfort in the knowledge that most teens *aren't* experimenting with illicit substances.

Talk to your daughter about drugs and alcohol

Your first line of defence against your daughter making poor decisions with drugs and alcohol is open communication. Drugs will be a topic of discussion between your daughter and her friends, but a lot of what she learns from her peers will be incorrect. You can help her have the right information, but only if she comes to you with questions. Whether or not she does will depend on your approach, so plan your conversations carefully.

Talk to your daughter about drugs and alcohol so you can gain a better understanding of what she knows about drugs and her views on drug use in people her age. Start by asking if she's ever been indirectly exposed to drugs and alcohol or if she knows anyone who's experimented with drugs. Seek out her thoughts on the risks involved with this. Listen to her answers and ask questions that will help you understand her opinions. If she admits to having friends who experiment with drugs or if her attitude towards drugs seems a little blasé, avoid going along with your urge to lecture her and don't put her on the spot by wanting to know which of her friends has experimented. If your goal is to open the door for future conversations, being confrontational won't help you achieve this. How you approach this initial conversation will determine how influential you can be in guiding your daughter's decisions, so choose your words wisely.

If your teen doesn't seem to have a good understanding of the dangers of experimenting with drugs, present her with accurate information but be careful not to exaggerate. Don't convey your anxiety about the issue, and don't be too transparent about your agenda to convince her to abstain from drug use. If you're too emphatic, she'll think you're over-reacting and she won't take your warnings seriously. Stick to the facts and stay neutral.

If you don't know where to start, start by talking with her about the effects of different types of drugs. Explain that how a drug affects someone will depend on the type of drug and how much of a drug they take; the person's size, weight and health; and whether that person has any other drugs (prescription or otherwise) in their system. It's

Cigarettes, alcohol, and drug use in teens

	Percentage using				Percentage not using			
	Australia:[1] 12–17 years	United States:[2] 8th, 10th, 12th grade	England:[3] 11–15 years	United Kingdom:[4] 15–16 years	Australia:[1] 12–17 years	United States:[2] 8th, 10th, 12th grade	England:[3] 11–15 years	United Kingdom:[4] 15–16 years
Cigarettes	2%[a]	19%[a]	19%[a]	23%[b]	98%[a]	81%[a]	81%[a]	77%[b]
Alcohol	22%[a]	42%[a]	44%[a]	65%[b]	78%[a]	58%[a]	56%[a]	35%[b]
Cannabis	12%[c,d]	23%[c]	8%[c]	25%[a]	88%[c,d]	77%[c]	92%[c]	75%[a]
Other illicit drugs	9%[c]	10%[c]	15%[c]	9%[a]	91%[c]	90%[c]	85%[c]	91%[a]

1 Australian Institute of Health and Welfare 'National Drug Strategy Household Survey Web Report 2016', Canberra: AIHW.
2 'Monitoring the Future: National results on adolescent drug use 2016', The University of Michigan Institute for Social Research.
3 'Smoking, Drinking and Drug Use Among Young People in England Survey 2016', England: NHS Digital.
4 European School Survey Project on Alcohol and Other Drugs 2011.

a Figure based on lifetime use.
b Figure based on use in last 30 days.
c Figure based on use in last 12 months.
d Figure based on data from 14 to 19-year-old participants.

important for her to know that a drug can affect how aware someone is of what's happening around them and how quickly they can react to a situation. Explain that these effects will pass, but highlight that they can be problematic should that person find themselves in a dangerous situation.

It's also important to talk to your daughter about drug lacing. She needs to know that recreational drugs are often made more dangerous by the addition of other substances. Sometimes other additives are cut into a drug to enhance or alter its effects, but often it's done to sell cheaper drugs in the place of something more expensive to maximize profits. Draw your daughter's attention to the fact that because recreational drugs are illegal, there's no regulatory body to monitor how the drugs are made or what's in them. What this means is that when someone experiments with recreational drugs, they can't be sure of exactly what they're taking or the strength of the mixture. They're taking a gamble, not just with their physical health, but their safety as well.

Once you've said your piece, tell your daughter that you trust her to make a good decision and let her know that she's welcome to come to you with questions or advice any time she likes. Your anxiety will make you want to keep talking so you can reinforce just how dangerous drugs can be, but keep in mind that less is sometimes more. The more you talk, the more she'll feel like you're trying to control her and the less she'll listen.

There's no one thing you can say that will keep your daughter from experimenting with drugs and alcohol. Remember, your objective is to open the door for future communication, not to try to control her decision because that won't work. Plant your seeds of information and leave your teen to think on them. Trust her to use the information you've given her wisely.

Talking to your teen about drugs: common pitfalls to avoid

When it comes to drugs and alcohol, how much of your advice gets listened to will depend on your approach, so plan your conversation ahead of time and avoid the common pitfalls outlined for you below.

Parent: Have you got a minute? I want to speak to you about a few concerns I have.

Teen: (*frustrated*) Right now? We're meant to be leaving. You said you'd drop me at 6 pm.

Starting big conversations when your teen's in a rush isn't a good move. She'll be frustrated by your timing and less likely to listen to what you have to say.

Parent: Will anyone be drinking at the party tonight? Will you be drinking? Will there be drugs?

Teen: (*feeling even more frustrated*) What? Where is this coming from?

A barrage of questions will make your teen feel like she's being interrogated. Direct questions like this will also put your teen on edge, and she'll be less open to having a frank and honest conversation with you as a result.

Parent: I just think that now you're going to parties more, you need to be aware of drink spiking and things like that. There was a really sad story on the news last week, a girl your age died after taking drugs at a concert. I've heard so many stories from other parents as well, about kids getting themselves into awful situations when they've had too much to drink. Did you know a girl at your school was sexually assaulted a few years ago at a party?

Teen: (*struggling to stay composed*) Mum, I'm not going to a rave, I'm going to a party with a few friends at Claire's house. No one's going to be doing drugs or drinking; well, none of my friends will be drinking anyway.

If you're too emphatic about the dangers of drug use, you'll lose your teen. Avoid jumping straight to worst-case scenarios and stick to general, factual information instead.

Parent: What do you mean, 'none of your friends anyway'. Who do you know that's drinking at these parties? Do their parents know they're drinking? Who's supplying them with alcohol? You're all underage for heavens' sake!

Teen: (*losing interest and tuning out*) I don't know, Mum. I'm just trying to be honest. I haven't spoken to every single person going to the party, so I don't know if anyone will be drinking. I can't control what other people do. If other people drink I can't stop them, but that doesn't mean I'm going to join in.

Don't lose sight of your objective — opening the lines of communication between you and your teen. She's not going to out her friends, she'll lie if she has to, and because you've made her uncomfortable, you've as good as guaranteed she won't come to you for advice in the future, even if she really needs to.

Parent: If you ever do drink or take something, you'll be grounded for the remainder of your teenage years. Don't forget that. Let's go.

Look for opportunities to give your teen positive feedback, for example: 'I forget how mature you are sometimes. You're absolutely right. You can't control what other people do; it's what you do that's important. If other people drink that's on them, it's not your job to police their decisions.' And don't end your conversation on a negative note. Leaving things on a negative note will make future conversations less likely.

Negotiate clear limits and a specific plan for party attendance

Beyond giving her the facts, you can also help your teen make the right choices by establishing a specific plan ahead of time. Know where your teen is going and set a curfew for pick-up. You'll want her home as early as possible, and she'll want to stay out as late as she can, so negotiate a reasonable compromise.

Ask for the name and number of the parent/s hosting the party and let your teen know that you'll call the supervising parents to introduce yourself. Your teen won't like this because it's an unwanted reminder that she's not as independent as she'd like to be, and she'll try to convince you not to call. She'll argue that it's weird for you to call the supervising parents and tell you you're over-reacting, but don't take the bait. Calling the host parents will help you confirm that: (1) there is a party; (2) the host parents know about the party and will be present; and (3) alcohol won't be provided. It also means a parent at the party has your contact details if they need to get in touch for any reason, and the host parent/s will appreciate the call.

If your daughter refuses to give you parent contact details and forbids you to call, let her know that you're happy for her to go to the party, but you need to speak to the host parent/s first. If she refuses to budge, tell her that you'll leave it with her to make a decision, but if she's not happy for you to call, the party is unfortunately off the table. Her resistance might be a symptom of her frustration at not being given the level of freedom she'd like, but strong resistance might also mean she's hiding something. Your teen might know there won't be any parents at the party, she might not have been honest with you about who else is going, or the party might be a cover for other plans she knows you won't agree to. Stand your ground. It's hard to be the bad guy, but safety trumps everything.

Make sure your teen has a way to get to and from the party. If you're driving, negotiate a drop-off point. You might feel rude dropping your teen off without saying hello and thank you to the host parents, but the idea of you escorting her in will horrify your daughter. Don't take this personally. If she's happy for you to walk her in, great, but if she's not, respect her wishes and be comfortable knowing you've spoken to the host parents ahead of time.

If your daughter has organized a lift with a friend's parent, call this parent to confirm they're happy to be the designated driver. Have an agreement in place that she'll call or text you if the location of the party changes, so you know where she is at all times, and if she plans to stay the night at a friend's house after the party, call and check this plan with her friend's parent and offer to return the favour next time. Other parents will appreciate your call, and good communication will help you stay a step ahead of any suspect plans.

Negotiation: putting it into practice

The teenage version of your daughter is different from the younger, more agreeable version, but you can help her to be less argumentative by switching to a collaborative parenting approach. Consider the following scenario. Your daughter wants to go to a party at the weekend and she's pushing to be picked up later than you'd like. A collaborative approach to limit-setting might look something like this:

Teen: But *everyone* is going. You can't pick me up at 9.30 pm, it'll be so embarrassing.

Parent: Okay, I can understand you're worried about having to leave earlier than everyone else. What do you think is a reasonable time for me to pick you up?

Teen: Midnight?

Parent: That's a little later than I was thinking. Remember, you've got netball first thing in the morning and I've got to get up and drive you to that as well. I don't want too late a night.

Teen: Can't I just get an Uber when I'm ready to come home?

Parent: I'm not really comfortable with that. At sixteen, I don't like the idea of you getting in a car with a stranger by yourself. How about I pick you up at 10.30 pm?

Teen: 10.45 pm?

Parent: Really, the extra fifteen minutes is that important? Okay, 10.45 pm but you'll need to be ready to leave at 10.45 pm on the dot and if you're not, I won't be so willing to compromise on the extra fifteen minutes next time. I'm sure you'll be ready on time and it won't be a problem. I'm just letting you know what I'm thinking so we're both on the same page.

Of course, real-life conversations rarely run as smoothly as this, and eye rolls and exaggerated sighs will probably be part of the mix, but don't let that distract you. Stay focused on the task at hand. Ask your daughter for her input, show her you understand her concerns, and be as flexible as you can — within reason — with your limits. If she reverts to being argumentative, stay calm and keep the conversation on track. Remember, negotiation is a new skill for both of you, and practice makes perfect.

Follow through with planned consequences

Make it clear to your teen ahead of time that there will be consequences for her not sticking to the agreed plan, and be specific; knowing exactly what's at risk will help her to make better decisions. For consequences to be effective they also need to be meaningful, so think about what sorts of consequences will be significant enough to make your teen take notice. Telling her that any deviations from your agreed plan will result in 48 hours of no TV is a weak consequence if your daughter doesn't spend much time watching TV anyway. Telling her a breach will mean 48 hours without her phone, on the other hand, may be a different story.

If your teen is responsible and meets all your expectations, make sure you let her know that you're proud of her, and reinforce that when she shows you she can be responsible it's a reminder to you that she's ready for more independence. If she fails to stick to the plans you agreed on, whether by getting home late or not being where she said she'd be, follow through. Consequences will only be effective if your daughter knows you mean business. Setting consequences and not following through teaches her that you don't really mean what you say, and this undercuts your parenting power. Your teen will be annoyed with you for enforcing consequences, but her distress will remind her to make a better decision next time.

Help your daughter develop exit strategies

Your final line of defence against drug and alcohol experimentation involves exit strategies. Your daughter's immature brain will make it hard for her to think clearly and make good decisions on the spot, but you can influence her choices by helping her to problem-solve ahead of time. Ask your teen if she's thought about what she would do if a friend offered her drugs, and how she could say no if she needed to. Ask her if she can think of any situations where it would be harder to say no — such as if a boy she liked offered her drugs, or if one of the popular girls asked her to join them — and help her think of solutions for this. Likewise, help her brainstorm ideas for how she might get out of a situation she didn't feel

83

comfortable in, such as a party that started to get out of hand, or plans she didn't feel right about.

Conversations like this are also an opportunity to reinforce to your teen that she can call you anytime she needs to. It's important that she knows your expectations, but she also needs to know that if she's ever in trouble, regardless of what rules she broke to get herself into the situation, you're someone she can call for help.

What to do when you catch your daughter out

If at some point you bust your teen for drinking or experimenting with drugs, speak her language. Raging at her for her stupidity might make you feel better initially, but it won't necessarily motivate her to make a different decision next time. Making a change to her freedom and independence will.

Take Jaqueline and Katie, for example. Both girls recently snuck out at night to attend a party they'd been told they weren't allowed to go to, and both experimented with alcohol. Jacqueline hasn't done anything like this before, but Katie's snuck out a few times now to go drinking. More times, in fact, than her parents know. When Jacqueline's parents learnt she'd gone to the party without their permission — another parent saw a photo of Jacqueline at the party, drinking, on her daughter's Facebook feed — they were furious and grounded her for a month. Katie's parents weren't impressed either, but they were a bit more lenient. They spoke to Katie at length about how disappointed they were, and threatened to ground her if it happened again, but that was the worst of it — no other action was taken.

Jacqueline didn't enjoy being grounded, and was particularly annoyed at having to miss out on a party she'd been looking forward to for weeks, but she tolerated her consequence well, knowing she'd done the wrong thing. She definitely didn't sneak out again — she knew it would only make things worse — and she hasn't experimented with alcohol again since.

Katie, on the other hand, still hasn't learnt her lesson. She's continued to drink and sneak out to parties she knows she's not allowed to go to, but she's careful not to get caught. On the rare occasion she's found out, she suffers through a lengthy lecture, but nothing her parents say seems to stick. They're fast getting sick of her complete disregard for their household rules.

> I don't know why she's being so disrespectful. We say yes to most things she asks for and we're pretty flexible with curfew, so why she feels the need to sneak out is beyond me. And that's not even the worst of it. We've spoken to her about alcohol so many times and asked her not to drink — she's much too young — but she doesn't seem to care. Sure, she's apologetic when she gets caught and promises not to do it again, but then a few months later we're back at square one. Last week was the last straw. I picked her up from a party like we'd agreed, and I could tell she'd been drinking. Not so much that she was sick, but enough to be tipsy and louder than usual. I couldn't believe it — she knew I was picking her up and she had a few drinks anyway! She's not listening to us and I really don't know what else to do.

Katie's not listening to her parents because what they're saying isn't meaningful to her. Yes, she has to endure a longwinded lecture when she's caught breaking household rules, but a lecture isn't compelling enough to motivate her to change her behaviour. And because her parents only ever threaten to ground her without ever following through, none of what they say really carries much weight anyway.

If Katie's parents want her to listen, they're going to need to start speaking a language Katie understands: limited freedom.

Use consequences to teach your teen to say no

If your teen makes a misguided decision and experiments with drugs or alcohol, tell her that her decision has made you question whether she's mature enough to be responsible, and because of this you'll need to put a few additional measures in place until she's able to demonstrate that she can make responsible decisions. What this looks like will differ from teen to teen and will depend on the circumstances, but possible measures to consider are: a ban on socializing outside school hours for a set period of time; an earlier curfew; restrictions around the types of social events she's able to attend; and stricter rules around communication and parent check-ins when she's out with friends (e.g. your teen texting you at intervals to let you know she's safe). Your daughter will hate you impinging on her freedom, but that's exactly why she'll make more considered decisions in the future.

If you do end up needing to set limits around your daughter's freedom, it's important to also establish a clear plan for how she can earn back her independence. How quickly this occurs and the nature of this plan will also depend on the circumstances, but as an example, the first week of your plan might include your daughter not being allowed to attend any social events; the second week might see you agree to her attending a small gathering with parental supervision and an earlier curfew; and in later weeks she might be able to attend social activities as usual but with more regular text communication. It means more work in the short-term, but a gradual re-introduction of her independence is important because it helps to reinforce that her freedom is contingent on demonstrations of her ability to make good decisions.

The important bits

+ When she starts high school, your daughter will start to be exposed to drugs and alcohol.
+ Not allowing her to attend parties will limit her exposure, but it won't help your daughter develop the skills she needs to say no if she needs to.
+ DO talk to your teen about drugs and alcohol and help her to understand the risks.
+ DON'T be too emphatic in your approach or your teen will think you're exaggerating and she won't listen to what you have to say.
+ DO help your daughter brainstorm and plan ahead for problem situations.
+ DO have the right scaffolding in place to help your daughter make sensible decisions.
+ DO set clear limits and communicate with other parents to help minimize your daughter's risk for poor decision-making.
+ DO make your daughter aware of what consequences you'll enforce if she experiments with drugs and alcohol.
+ DO follow through with consequences if you need to. Not following through teaches your daughter that she doesn't need to listen to what you say.
+ DO make your daughter's freedom contingent on a demonstration of her ability to make good decisions.

7

WHEN YOUR DAUGHTER'S STRUGGLING WITH BODY CONFIDENCE

There's a body image crisis unfolding amongst teenage girls. Far too many girls are unhappy with the way they look and they're desperate to change their appearance. They feel self-conscious about the size of their thighs, embarrassed by the shape of their hips, and would give anything for a flatter stomach and a smaller waist. Even more concerning is the level of importance teenage girls attach to their appearance. They aspire to be thin not just because they'd like to look this way, but because they believe they *need* to look this way. To them, it's not enough to be funny, intelligent and compassionate, because these qualities aren't valued commodities. Their body shape and weight define their self-worth, because they've been taught — by Hollywood, the media and the fashion industry — that skinny is pretty and thin is the pathway to happiness.

And while an alarming number of teenage girls are developing eating disorders, it's not just teens with eating disorders who struggle with their body image. For the last decade, Dove has been committed to researching the self-esteem and body confidence of women and girls across the globe. The results of their research have been heartbreaking to read. Body image issues are commonplace, but women in Australia, the United Kingdom and the United States are among the least body confident in the world. In the United States, only 24 per cent of women see their bodies in a positive light, and this percentage is even smaller in Australia and the United Kingdom (20 per cent in both countries). The body confidence of teens (aged 10–17 years) isn't much better. According to Dove's research:

+ only 11 per cent of girls globally feel comfortable describing themselves as beautiful
+ 80 per cent admit to opting out of important life activities such as time with friends or club try-outs when they don't feel good about their appearance
+ 70 per cent of teens have said they find it hard to express their opinions and stick to decisions when they feel unhappy with the way they look
+ 72 per cent feel overwhelmed by social pressure to be beautiful
+ 70 per cent have confessed to dietary restriction or otherwise, putting their health at risk to try to change their appearance.[1]

So many teens have a negative body image that it's easy to fall into the trap of dismissing body dissatisfaction as a normal phase of adolescence. But rather than alleviate our anxiety, the prevalence of body image issues should increase our concern. Body image is a serious issue that needs to be addressed, which begs the question — what's behind the low body confidence epidemic unfolding among teenage girls?

Why are teens so dissatisfied with their bodies?

The media has garnered a lot of attention for its role in the current body image crisis, and for good reason. Teens are bombarded with images of stick-thin models with the 'perfect' body — slender limbs, a flat stomach and a tiny waist — and they're cheated into believing they should look this way too; but it's an unrealistic ideal. In reality, images are retouched and digitally altered, and the models teens see are often unnaturally thin and not representative of the appearance of teens in general. But teens forget this. They get stuck on the difference between what they're told they should look like and what they actually look like, and they learn to dislike their bodies.

Especially compelling evidence for the contribution of the media to body dissatisfaction in teens comes from research exploring the relationship between the two in populations protected from Western influences. Dr Anne Becker, a Maude and Lillian Presley Professor of Global Health and Social Medicine at Harvard Medical School, is famous for her research in this area. She focused her research on the eating behaviours and attitudes of Fijian teens after noticing the different standards of beauty valued by Fijian people and the incongruousness of diets and weight loss to the Fijian culture. Unlike in Western cultures, larger, more robust body shapes are traditionally admired by Fijians for their association with wealth, fertility and an ability to work.[2]

What also made Fiji unique at the time of Dr Becker's research was the country's lack of exposure to Western media. Television wasn't accessible in Fiji until 1995, so prior to this Fijian teens were largely protected from Western influences and Western standards of beauty. This meant Dr Becker and her team were able to assess the eating behaviours and attitudes of Fijian teens both before and after the introduction of Western media. Their findings were interesting. Despite only one case of anorexia nervosa having been reported in Fiji prior to 1995, key indicators of disordered eating, including self-induced vomiting and an increased interest in dieting and weight loss, were significantly more prevalent among teenage girls by 1998, just three years after the introduction of television. Eleven per cent of teens admitted to purging to lose weight (something unheard of prior to television exposure), 69 per cent admitted to dieting to lose weight, 74 per cent said they felt 'too big or fat' and were more likely to diet as a result, and 40 per cent said they wanted to lose weight because they thought being thinner would increase their career prospects.

But the media isn't the only factor at play. A study led by Alison Field, Professor of Paediatrics at Harvard Medical School, found that after media influences, peer influences are the second strongest predictor of body dissatisfaction in teenage girls, followed by parent modelling of negative body-image messages.[3] Intrinsic factors can also play a role. Studies show, for example, that teens who routinely engage in body comparisons — a comparison between a teen's own body shape and weight and the body shape and weight of others — are also more likely to develop a negative body image. Social media certainly hasn't helped in this regard. Body comparisons are no longer contained to real-world interactions; Facebook and Instagram provide platforms for digital comparisons as well. Teens scrutinize photos of themselves online, fixating on their own perceived imperfections and flaws and obsessing over the 'perfect' appearance of their friends, friends of friends, and friends of friends of friends. And then there's the ever helpful 'thinspiration' and 'fitspiration' accounts that so many teens follow on social media. These accounts supposedly encourage a fit and healthy approach to life, but obsessing over diet and exercise isn't healthy, and neither is exposure to 'inspirational' quotes such as 'All of the pain you go through today will be worth it on the scales tomorrow', or 'Eat junk. Look like junk. Eat clean. Look lean.' They're toxic messages to insecure young girls who are still learning to be body confident.

Toxic messages on social media

Social media is a great platform for social connectedness, but it's also a platform for the promotion of unhealthy trends that can affect the body image of teenage girls. A few trends are listed for you below, but trends change rapidly so it's worthwhile doing your own research and being aware of the accounts your daughter follows.

The box gap: A box gap is the gap you can see between a girl's thighs when she's standing up and her feet and knees are pressed together. Not everyone has a box gap, but they're admired and seen as something to be proud of on social media.

The ab crack: A more recent trend, the ab crack is the vertical line running down the length of the torso seen on most bikini models. It's the newest standard of beauty on social media.

The bikini bridge: This is the term used to describe the space between a teen's bathing suit bottoms and her hip bones when she lies down. This trend has been around since 2014 and, like the box gap, bikini bridges are well liked on social media.

The A4 challenge: This challenge encourages teens to see if their waists are smaller than an A4 sheet of paper. Teens who succeed at this challenge are admired for their level of thinness.

The collarbone challenge: This challenge stems from the belief that the skinnier you are, the more pronounced your collarbones should be, and the more coins you should be able to balance in the space above them. It's a disturbing measure of beauty.

The belly button challenge: This challenge encourages teens to reach one arm behind their back and around their waist and stomach, to see if they can touch their belly button. Not being able to do this is considered an indication of the need for weight loss.

How do we fix the body image crisis?

The body image epidemic affecting teenage girls needs to be addressed, but how? Social media and the Internet make it virtually impossible for you to shield your daughter against images promoting an unrealistic body ideal, and little's being done at a government level to enforce responsible advertising. Australia is a perfect example. In 2009, Australian MP Kate Ellis, then Minister for Youth and Sport, appointed a National Advisory Group on Body Image — made up of media, fashion and eating disorder experts — to encourage advertisers, the media and the fashion industry to promote positive body image messages. Among their many recommendations, the advisory group suggested that more be done to diversify the body shapes and sizes of models used in the media and fashion industries, with a particular focus on not using models of an unhealthy weight, and asked industries to commit to not digitally altering images in a way that promotes an unrealistic and unhealthy body image. It was a well-intentioned initiative, but a voluntary one. Without legislation to force compliance, few organizations adopted the advisory board's recommendations, and as Mia Freedman, the chair of the advisory group, has herself acknowledged, 'Nothing has changed'; magazines are still digitally altering their images and models still aren't representative of the body shape and weight of the average teenage girl.

At an international level, there have been a few more promising initiatives. In 2006, Spain and Italy both took steps to ban unhealthily thin models from participating in premiere fashion shows. Going a step further, in 2012 the Israeli government passed a law banning the use of models with a Body Mass Index (BMI) of 18.5 or less and requiring clear labelling of Photoshopped images in magazines and advertisements. The 'Photoshop' law was the first of its kind in the world and has inspired action in other countries. Most recently, France passed its own laws prohibiting the use of unhealthily thin models and demanding the use of clear labelling for digitally altered images — but they added penalties. Under these new laws, French agencies who fail to disclose image retouching will be hit with a fine of €37,500, and those who employ models without the required doctor's certificate verifying their overall health and healthy BMI may be subjected to a fine of €75,000 and six months in jail.

Despite these positive initiatives, we're still a long way from a cure; but while the negative body image messages teens are exposed to via magazines, TV and social media are largely out of your control, you're not powerless. What you can control are the body image lessons your teen learns from you. You have the power to give her a strong counter-message.

When should I be worried?

Teens with a negative body image are at higher risk for eating disorders, depression, low self-esteem, binge eating and other unhealthy weight control behaviours. Not all teens who struggle with body image will develop an eating disorder, but if your teen starts to show signs of low body confidence, watch her diet and exercise closely. Your daughter might not open up to you about her insecurities, so be on the lookout for warning signs of a negative body image like the ones listed for you below:

+ body bashing (critical self-talk about her appearance)
+ obsessing over appearance and specific body parts

+ being fixated on weight loss
+ fussy eating and/or rigid exercise routines driven by a desire to lose weight
+ body comparisons (your daughter comparing her own body shape and weight to the body shape and weight of others)
+ your teen not wanting to participate in activities because of the way she looks
+ distress over comments about her appearance
+ taking an excessive amount of time to get ready for social events.

Focus on function, not appearance

Your daughter will get drawn into focusing on what her body looks like, but you can help her switch her focus so she sees her body for what it is: a complex and pretty amazing machine.

So much of what her body does happens without her awareness, like breathing. She won't notice, but she'll take twelve to twenty breaths every minute. That's anywhere from 17,000 to almost 30,000 breaths each day. For every breath, the respiratory control centre in her brain will instruct specialized groups of muscles to contract and relax to draw in and expel air from her lungs, while sensors in her brain and blood vessels monitor her oxygen and carbon dioxide levels so that changes can be made to her rate of breathing. It's a complicated process with lots of moving parts, but it's executed seamlessly. So seamlessly, in fact, that she isn't even aware it's happening. And that pretty much sums up your daughter's body. It's a quiet achiever. It works discreetly in the background to make sure she has everything she needs to be healthy, happy and able; but its quiet efficiency means it's easy for her to get distracted by her appearance and overlook what her body does for her. You can help her avoid this trap.

Teach your daughter to appreciate her body by encouraging her to prioritize treating it well. When it comes to diet, encourage your daughter to eat a healthy, balanced diet so that her body is nourished and has enough energy to fuel all its important functions (see Chapter 3, 'When your daughter wants to diet' for more on this). Encourage her to exercise so her body will be fit, strong and healthy; help her to prioritize sleep so that her body gets the rest it needs to function at its best; and don't let her forget to thank her body for all its hard work by making time for body self-care (think massages, bubble baths and body lotions). Her body will carry her through the rest of her life; teach her to respect it.

Throw out your bathroom scales

Your daughter will have a healthier body image if she steers clear of bathroom scales. Weight loss isn't a solution for low body confidence and trying to achieve a positive body image this way will only keep your daughter stuck. Her quest to change her body will consume her and reinforce her misperception that her appearance and weight are her most important features, more important even than who she is and what she's capable of. When she doesn't lose weight as quickly as she'd like, she'll beat herself up and feel hopeless about ever feeling good about her body, and because her weight isn't really the cause of her insecurities, if she does manage to lose the weight she still won't be happy, because it's her attitude towards her body that needs to change, not her body shape and weight.

If your daughter's in a healthy weight range, discourage any attempts at weight loss and throw out your bathroom scales. If she's not in a healthy weight range and needs to lose weight, encourage her to exercise and eat healthily, but avoid linking either to weight loss and discourage weight monitoring. Suggest she eats better quality food so she can have more energy, and help her find non-weight related motivations for exercise, like fitness, strength or health. Regular exercise and healthy eating will help her lose the weight she needs to be healthy, without the unhealthy fixation on weight loss that will undermine her body confidence.

Encourage positive body talk

Encouraging your daughter to have a positive attitude towards her body will be a challenge. If she has a negative body image she'll readily identify what she doesn't like about her body, but find it harder to identify things she does like about her appearance. She'll compare herself to her friends and think everyone around her is skinnier, prettier and more attractive than she is, and she'll wish she had a flatter stomach, smaller thighs and a prettier face. She'll find compliments about her appearance hard to take seriously because they're inconsistent with how she sees herself, and when *you* give her compliments she'll dismiss them on the assumption that your love for her is blinding you to her imperfections, or because she thinks you're giving her a false compliment to trick her into feeling better. Don't let her dismissiveness deter you. She may not hear you at first, but learning to accept your compliments about her appearance will help to correct your daughter's negative body image bias. It might feel like complimenting her appearance works against your end-goal of minimizing this as a focus, but if your appearance-focused compliments are intermixed with compliments about her personal strengths and capabilities, it won't. If your balance is right, she'll develop a healthy relationship with her body *and* understand she's more than her appearance.

Be a good positive body image model

One of the most powerful means you have at your disposal to help your daughter develop a positive body image, is having a positive relationship with your own body. The negative body talk that plays out in the privacy of your head may seem relatively innocuous, but your thoughts will become your actions and your actions are noticeable to everyone, including your daughter. Take Louise, for example. Louise has presented with concerns about her daughter's body image.

> I'm so worried about her. She seems so self-conscious and she doesn't need to be. She's a healthy weight — she's definitely not model thin, but she's not big, either — but I can tell she's unhappy. She used to love going shopping for clothes, and I now have to pull out all the stops to convince her to come with me. And any time she has a party to go to it's such a drama. She spends hours getting ready, and there's tears and tantrums along the way because she thinks she looks gross and can't find an outfit that hides her 'fat thighs'. She doesn't have fat thighs — I've told her that a hundred times — but nothing I say seems to help.
>
> My mother was so critical of my appearance when I was growing up and it really affected me. I've always been so careful not to say anything remotely negative to Haley about her body, and I never talk about my own appearance in front of her — I know how damaging that can be — but I'm worried about how critical she is of herself. I don't want her to have the struggles I did with my body.

Louise thinks she's protecting Haley from her own body image issues, but Haley's picking up on more than she realizes …

> My mum is such a hypocrite. She's always going on about how I'm perfect just the way I am, and how I don't need to lose weight, but she's skinnier than me and she's always exercising and on some kind of diet. She was doing some kind of cleanse last week — something about toxins or whatever — but I know she was doing it because she was freaking out that she'd eaten so much while we were on holidays; I'm not stupid. She's always so strict with what she eats. She buys us biscuits and things for snacks but never eats any of them herself, and I know it's because she thinks it all goes straight to her thighs because I hear her talking to her friends about it. And then she lectures me about how I should love and respect my body and not try to change it! I honestly think she's the one who needs to see you, not me.

And while there's no getting around the fact that mums have a bigger influence than dads when it comes to the body image of teenage girls, dads, don't get complacent. What you do matters too, just ask Hannah.

> My dad is *obsessed* with running and fitness. He's always trying to get me to go for runs with him and he's really annoying about it. He keeps telling me he wants me to run so I can be outdoors more, but the other day I overheard him telling Mum he's worried I'm 'too big'.

Word for word that's what he said: 'Do you think she's getting too big?' I'm only a size small!

All he ever talks about since he started running is his weight. He's obsessed with being at a good race weight. You'd think he was training for the Olympic team, not a 10-kilometre fun run. And he goes on and on about all the things we should and shouldn't eat. I had three pieces of toast for afternoon tea yesterday; I know that sounds like a lot but I didn't get to eat much for lunch and I was hungry, and he came into the kitchen, stood there and watched me eat, then said: 'Do you think you really need that?'

He's not always like that and sometimes he says nice things to me, but I'm starting to think I need to be doing more to stay on top of my weight. Maybe everyone thinks I'm getting fat and they're just too nice to tell me?

You can say all the right things and tell your daughter that the size and shape of her body isn't important, but if you're meticulous with what you eat and take a weight-loss approach to exercise, it weakens her confidence in your counsel that appearance isn't important. Likewise, if she overhears you making body comparisons or complaining about your big thighs/wide hips/flabby arms/wobbly stomach, it undoes everything you've tried to teach her about body acceptance and loving her body.

As part of their commitment to helping girls and women develop a positive relationship with their bodies, Dove put together a video a few years ago titled 'Dove Legacy' — it's powerful and worth a watch. In the video, mums are asked to describe the things they like and dislike about their bodies. Separately, their daughters are also asked the same question. What's interesting is the extent to which girls mirror the body image of their mothers. The girls in the video dislike the parts of their body that their mothers identify as their least favourite body part, but they've internalized positive body image messages from their mothers as well. For example, one mum says she tries to focus on the fact that her legs — a part of her body she dislikes — are strong and help her to be a good runner, and her daughter lists her legs as a body part she likes because they're good for running.

When it comes to body image, if you don't practice what you preach, neither will your daughter. Lead by example and make working on your own body image part of your parenting plan.

The important bits

+ An alarming number of teenage girls have a negative body image.
+ A negative body image increases the risk of teens developing eating disorders, depression, low self-esteem, binge eating and other unhealthy weight control behaviours.
+ The media, social media and body image messages from family and friends are all significant contributors to a teen's body image.
+ The unrealistic images your teen will be exposed to via magazines, TV and social media are largely out of your control, but you can control the body image messages she receives from you at home.
+ Dads, DON'T leave body image parenting to mums — get involved.
+ DO help your daughter focus on what her body can do, not just what it looks like.
+ DO teach your daughter to treat her body well with regular exercise, a healthy diet, sufficient sleep and self-care.

+ DO get rid of your bathroom scales and discourage weight monitoring.
+ DO help your daughter learn to see her body positively by giving her appearance-based compliments.
+ DO work on having a positive relationship with your own body so you can be a positive body image role model for your daughter.
+ DON'T model a negative body image by being body critical and focused on weight.

8

WHEN YOUR DAUGHTER'S WARDROBE STARTS TO CHANGE

In her younger years, your daughter might have been desperate to wear pretty dresses, pink headbands and glittery T-shirts, but fast forward a few years and my how things have changed. The sparkles and glitter are gone, and in their place are cringeworthy low-cut jeans, short shorts, and midriff-baring crop tops.

Your daughter's experimentation with fashion — if you can call it that — will make your head spin: there's the attention you're worried she'll attract from boys, your concern for her reputation and (if you're really honest) fear that *you'll* be judged negatively by other parents for the way your daughter dresses. But while these concerns are front and centre in your mind, they're not even on your daughter's radar.

Your daughter wants to be accepted by her peers; she wants to fit in, get noticed and be popular. She's seen her friends amass hundreds of likes for their near-nude selfies on Instagram and it's sparked her interest in short shorts and low-cut tops. Thanks to her gross over-exposure to advertisements featuring scantily-dressed teens in provocative poses, she's desensitized to the suggestiveness of revealing outfits and completely unaware of the inappropriateness of her wardrobe choices. When you tell her that her shorts are too short, she rolls her eyes and tells you you're over-reacting, because her shorts aren't any shorter than what her friends wear, and they're definitely no more revealing than the shorts she sees on models in shop windows.

Your daughter won't see her wardrobe as problematic, but if her outfits show more skin than they hide, it's an issue. Getting noticed might initially make her feel good, but when she seeks and receives attention for her appearance, it reinforces the toxic 'sexy is the new pretty and appearance is everything' message she receives from the media, and this increases her risk for low self-esteem and body image issues. A provocative wardrobe will also make her a target for lewd comments from boys and bitchy remarks from other girls. The negative effects of this will initially be offset by the burst of confidence she feels when she's in the spotlight, but ongoing scrutiny will make her question her worth and fracture her self-confidence.

What *not* to do if you want to be effective

Your daughter's wardrobe is a delicate topic of conversation with a number of potential minefields. Her choice of outfit may give the illusion of body confidence, but her body confidence is fragile at this age and she's highly sensitive to comments about her appearance. Other people's opinions, including yours (despite her attempts to make you think otherwise) strongly influence how she feels about herself, so how you phrase your objections is important.

Outfits that leave little to the imagination might make you cringe, but it's not helpful to draw her attention to the inappropriateness of her outfit by telling her she looks cheap. The words 'you look like a prostitute' definitely shouldn't leave your mouth. Your intention may be to help your daughter understand the impact of her wardrobe, but your words will leave her feeling angry, humiliated and unsure of herself. Think of it this way: if a sales assistant told you the outfit you'd tried on looked 'a little young' for you, would you be grateful for their honest feedback or embarrassed and self-conscious? Shaming your daughter might be effective insofar as it motivates her to change her outfit, but it can also have a damaging effect on her self-esteem and body image. As a general rule, avoid any 'slut' based references when talking to your daughter about her wardrobe.

A lot of parenting books will advise you to solve your wardrobe wars by telling your daughter what she can and can't wear. If you have a teenage daughter who diligently listens to your advice and does what you say without question, this approach will probably work. This teen is a rare gem — if you have one, cherish her. If you have a daughter who's fiercely independent and resistant to listening to anything you have to say, this approach *won't* work. Your teen will see your wardrobe regulations as an attack on her independence, and she'll sidestep your rules by sneaking in a wardrobe change after she's left the house.

Attempting to control your teen's wardrobe with rules alone won't work, but that doesn't mean you're powerless. You can regain authority with a different approach.

Talk to your teen about the power of her wardrobe ... effectively

There's no one 'right' way to talk to your daughter about her wardrobe. Your goal is to help her understand the consequences of her wardrobe without shaming her in the process, and there are a few different ways you can achieve this.

That said, there are certain things you need to *not* say if you want her to listen and take your guidance on board. 'Other people will think badly of you if you dress like that' is one of them. True as it may be, phrasing your argument this way will make your daughter think you're telling her to dress differently because you're worried about what other people think. She'll take issue with this and passionately argue for her right to express herself and the injustice of slut shaming, and you'll wonder how the hell a conversation about her wardrobe spun into a debate about women's rights. If you want her to understand the power of her wardrobe in shaping other people's opinions of her, you'll need to pitch your argument differently.

Tell her that you want to have a chat about her wardrobe and if she starts to get defensive, reassure her that you're not criticizing her, you just want to speak to her about the consequences of her wardrobe choices. At some point, she'll argue that other people should judge her for who she is and not what she wears, and when she does, use this as an opportunity to side with her. Tell her you agree, people *should* ignore her wardrobe and judge her only on her character, but humans are flawed and nudity is distracting. When a streaker runs across a sports stadium, people can't help but look — no one keeps watching the game. When a woman sunbathes topless at the beach, people stare. When women wear revealing outfits, it's hard not to notice.

The reality is, certain outfits are distracting. Make it clear that you're not talking about spaghetti straps on singlet tops or mid-thigh length shorts and skirts, or she'll think you're over-reacting. Give her specific examples so she knows exactly what you mean: shorts that aren't long enough to fully cover her butt cheeks, skirts so tight you can see the outline of her underwear, and see-through tops paired with brightly coloured push-up bras that amplify her cleavage. And make sure you stick to neutral descriptions like this and not general judgmental descriptions like 'slutty clothes'. If you're too disparaging, she'll tune out and refuse to listen to what you have to say just to spite you.

Your teen needs your help to understand that, like it or not, there are unwritten rules that dictate what teenage girls can and can't wear if they want to be judged on more than their appearance. She needs to realize that when she wears clothes that barely cover her body, it's hard for the people around her — male or female — to see past her naked skin, and therein lies the problem. When people are distracted by her near-nudity, they miss the opportunity to see what's really important: who she is and what she stands for. Help your teen to see that if she really wants to stand up for women's rights and be respected for more than her appearance, she needs to change her wardrobe. Dressing slightly more modestly will help other people to see her for who she is — funny, kind, intelligent, passionate, strong — and *this* is how she can teach people to be less focused on appearance.

Her wardrobe as a screening tool

'Wearing that sends a certain message to boys; you'll give them the wrong idea' is another argument to avoid. She'll instantly see it for what it is — you trying to subtly tell her she looks like a slut — and this will likely trigger an explosive argument. Avoid this issue by reframing your argument. Tell her instead that if used correctly, her wardrobe can be a powerful screening tool for weeding out crappy boyfriends and jerks who aren't worth her time.

Your daughter will deny dressing to impress boys until she's blue in the face, so sidestep this argument and tell her that whether she dresses to get noticed by boys on purpose or not, revealing outfits will draw attention from players — the boys who pretend to be interested in starting a relationship when they're really only interested in sex — and these guys aren't worth her time. They boys who notice her when she's in her girl-next-door clothes — *they're* boyfriend material. These guys will appreciate her for who she is, not just what she looks like. They may not be the most popular guys or the guys with the greatest stage presence, but they're definitely the guys most worthy of her attention.

Dad power

Having a male perspective can help your daughter better understand the intricacies of the relationship between her wardrobe and male attention, so dads, get involved. Share your wisdom and teach your daughter about the workings of the male brain. Your words will carry quite a bit of weight on boy-related issues, so make sure your daughter knows that while you want her to wear whatever she feels most confident in, you think she's too amazing to have her skin be the only thing other people notice about her. She'll need to hear this from you more than once, but what you say will matter.

Make conversations about your daughter's worth a regular part of your dialogue.

Dressing for comfort

Encouraging your teen to dress for comfort is another option if you need to address her wardrobe. Instead of drawing her attention to other people's perceptions of her, encourage her to think about which clothes *she* feels most comfortable in. Ask her whether a miniskirt will help her to feel relaxed and confident or self-conscious and insecure if it means she can't sit down without showing her underwear. Encourage her to think about whether her strapless top will allow her to switch off and enjoy the party or if it'll be an ongoing distraction if she has to constantly check it hasn't slipped.

Be prepared for your teen to seem indifferent and uninterested in your advice and resist the urge to keep talking to reinforce your point. If you're too emphatic in your approach your teen will tune out and your words will fall on deaf ears. Say your piece and then leave it. Trust that your teen will think more about what you've said in her own time.

Don't expect your teen to dress like you

Your daughter needs your help to make wardrobe choices that don't make her vulnerable to feedback that will negatively affect her self-esteem and body image, but she also needs freedom to develop her own personal style. If her shorts are too short and her tops too tight, you might need to step in and set firmer boundaries, but make sure the boundaries you set are motivated by a genuine need and not just your preference for her to dress in ways *you* like. You might not like jeans with rips in them or tops with the backs cut out, but if she does, and if her outfits are overall pretty tame, give her the freedom to express herself and develop her own sense of fashion.

What if my daughter's wardrobe continues to cause conflict?

If your daughter's outfits are deliberately promiscuous and she doesn't respond to your indirect attempts to encourage her to change, you might need to step in and set firmer boundaries. If you usually give her money for clothes, stop. If she buys promiscuous clothes with her own money, take her to return them. If this doesn't work either, think about why your daughter is so hell-bent on dressing the way she does. Is she deliberately pushing your buttons to punish you for something? Is she feeling suffocated by you and exercising her independence by deliberately dressing to spite you? Uncovering her motivation and addressing any underlying issues will help you to reach a truce.

The important bits

+ Thanks to her over-exposure to sexually suggestive images in the media, in your daughter's teenage years, short shorts and midriff-baring crop tops will likely be 'essentials' in her wardrobe.
+ Speaking to your daughter about her wardrobe is a delicate conversation, so choose your words wisely.
+ DON'T use negative language, such as words like 'slutty' and 'cheap', to shame your daughter into wardrobe changes.
+ DON'T go overboard with wardrobe dos and don'ts.
+ DO help your daughter to understand that, like it or not, people will judge her based on what she wears.
+ DO help her to see that boys who only notice her when she's in a short skirt aren't worth her time.
+ DO encourage her to make wardrobe choices based on comfort.
+ DON'T try to make your teen dress like you. Give her the freedom to develop her own personal style.

9

WHEN YOUR DAUGHTER GETS A BOYFRIEND (AND YOU'RE WORRIED ABOUT HER HAVING SEX)

When your daughter starts dating, sex stops being a distant hypothetical. When she brings home her first boyfriend and you catch them making out, alarm bells start to ring. The thought of your daughter having sex will be confronting on multiple levels. There's the apprehension you'll feel about her having sex for the wrong reasons or before she's ready, your worry about sexually transmitted infections and, god forbid, pregnancy. And then there's the uneasy feeling that grips the pit of your stomach when you're reminded that this is real; she's a teenager and she's about to start exploring her sexuality.

The fact that sex is one of the first decisions your teen will make that you have no control over — zip, nada, none — makes things even more uncomfortable. You can give yourself the illusion of control by forbidding her to date, banning boys from the house and hovering outside her bedroom door, but the reality is different. If your daughter decides she wants to have sex, she will, whether you're ready for her to be sexually active or not. She'll organize to have sex at a friend's house, find a way to sneak her boyfriend into the house when you're not home, or if it comes down to it, she'll have sex in the back seat of her boyfriend's car. She doesn't have to ask your permission and she doesn't have to talk to you about it first, which is why she needs you to start talking to her about sex sooner rather than later.

There's no getting around it, talking to your teen about sex is awkward. It's sex. She's your daughter. It's an uncomfortable topic of conversation. When sex gets put on the agenda in my office, there's always a subtle but definite shift in the conversational atmosphere. Pleasantries come to a halt, there's a long drawn out silence, and then:

> Well, we came home early the other night and, um, well, we saw, ah, she was in her room with her boyfriend and, well, they were both, um, well I couldn't see exactly, but it looked like they were quite, um, well they looked like they were about to, his shirt was off, and, ah, they were kissing pretty passionately [insert awkward cough].

At this point, the teen becomes intensely interested in the palms of her hands and silently begs me to give her a free pass out of the session; Mum shifts uncomfortably and looks hesitantly at her daughter, torn between urgently wanting my advice and the knowledge that her daughter's going to kill her for raising this in session in the first place; and the murderous look on Dad's face tells me he's not really all that keen on the idea of his little girl having sex, and she can as good as kiss her freedom goodbye for the foreseeable future, at least until Dad's had time to purchase a firearm.

I dread the question I know is coming next when parents raise sex in session: 'Can you talk to her and tell her she shouldn't be having sex?' Can I talk to her? Yes. Am I going to instruct her not to have sex? No. It's not my job to convince teens to abstain from sex, and as a parent, it's not your job either. It's normal to want to protect her from doing something she's not ready for, but you can't control her decision to have sex. You can talk to her about the dangers of unprotected sex and the arguments for and against waiting, but the decision to have sex is hers and hers alone. It doesn't matter how many rules you set or how many lectures you give, if she wants to have sex she will, with or without your consent.

When it comes to sex, the more you talk *at* your daughter the more irritated she'll feel by your lack of respect for her independence, and the less likely she'll be to listen to anything you have to say. She doesn't need a lecture; she needs a sounding board. She needs help to sort through her feelings about sex, and she needs someone to ask the right questions to get her thinking, so she can make a carefully considered decision about what she is and isn't ready for.

Is my teen having sex?

It's normal for your teen to not want to talk to you about her sex life. Her caginess around questions about sex might make you suspicious, but it's not necessarily a sign of sexual activity. To her, her sex life — non-existent or not — is private and none of your business. By refusing to answer your questions, she's setting a healthy boundary and letting you know questions about her sex life are off limits. You'll no doubt feel that as her parent you have the right to know if she's sexually active, but if she's old enough to consent to sex, you don't, and persisting with intrusive questions will only drive a wedge between you.

Rest assured, most teens don't start having sex until late adolescence. A report prepared by the Guttmacher Institute shows that on average, young people in the United States have sex for the first time at around seventeen. The report also showed that 56 per cent of teenage girls aged between fifteen and nineteen *hadn't* had sex — most because they thought it went against their religious or moral beliefs, or because they didn't feel they'd met the right person yet — and amongst sexually active teens, only 13 per cent had had their first sexual experience before the age of fifteen. Seventy-three per cent of sexually active teens had had sex for the first time with someone they were in a relationship with, 16 per cent had had their first sexual experience with someone they'd just met or someone who was a friend, and almost 80 per cent had used contraception the first time they had sex, most having used a condom.[1-4]

A similar picture exists in Australia. La Trobe University in Melbourne regularly conducts a national survey of the sexual health of Australian teens, and their most recent survey in 2013 showed that of the 2000 Year 10, 11 and 12 students surveyed, a large majority of students hadn't had sex. Sixty-nine per cent of teens had had some form of sexual experience — whether that be deep kissing, the touching of genitals, or oral sex — but only 34 per cent had had sexual intercourse. Of those teenage girls who had been sexually active, half were Year 12 students, and most had had sex with their current boyfriend. Worryingly, less than half had always used a condom, 20 per cent had had sex with three or more people in the last twelve months, and nearly 30 per cent said that they'd had sex when they didn't want to; most because they wanted to please their partner or because they'd had sex under the influence of alcohol.[5]

It's reassuring to know that most teens aren't sexually active, but what about the teens who are? That there are teenage girls who aren't protecting themselves against sexually transmitted infections is concerning, and so is the fact that teens are having sex when they don't really want to.

Sex is an awkward topic of conversation, but your daughter needs you to open the lines of communication. She needs your help to make considered decisions she won't later regret, and it all starts with her feeling comfortable enough to talk to you when she needs to.

Starting a conversation about sex

Only 36 per cent of the teens who participated in La Trobe University's National Survey of Australian Secondary Students and Sexual Health felt confident they could talk to their parents about sex. That's a concerning statistic. If teens aren't talking to their parents, who are they turning to for advice? Their equally uninformed and inexperienced friends?

Your daughter needs to know she can talk to you about sex. Offering to talk to her isn't enough, she has to feel comfortable enough to actually take you up on your offer. Direct questions about her sex life will make her wildly *un*comfortable, so resist the urge to put her on the spot and demand to know if she's sexually active. If she is having sex, she'll tell you she's not, just to bring the conversation to an end; and if she's not sexually active, the bluntness of your approach and her ensuing awkwardness will all but guarantee she won't be coming to you for advice about sex at any point in the near future.

Instead of asking direct, intrusive questions about her sex life, get your daughter talking with open-ended, indirect questions. Ask whether people in her school year are having sex, and whether people who are sexually active are sleeping with people they're in relationships with, people they've never met before, or people they're interested in but not dating yet. Ask her what she thinks about this. Ask her to tell you more about her friends' attitudes towards sex and ask whether she agrees or disagrees with their way of thinking. Ask what advice she'd give to a friend thinking about having sex for the first time, and for her thoughts

115

on whether the decision to have sex should be an individual one or a decision couples make together.

During conversations about sex, be mindful of your delivery. You may want your daughter to wait to have sex, but trying to control her decision will get you nowhere fast. She's not going to abstain from sex just because you tell her to, and if you're too pushy, she won't come to you for advice and help when she needs it. Consider your own friendships. Who are you more likely to turn to for help: the non-judgmental friend who listens and only offers their opinion when you ask, or the disapproving friend who likes the sound of their own voice and isn't backwards in coming forwards with what they think, whether you've asked for their advice or not? Indirect questions won't get you the information you really want, but they'll help your daughter to feel comfortable enough to start talking. If sex is something *you're* uncomfortable talking about, indirect questions can help to alleviate your discomfort as well.

Talk about pregnancy and STIs, but don't *only* talk about that

Your daughter needs to be aware of the potential risks of unprotected sex, but don't fall into the trap of only talking to her about sex in the context of pregnancy and sexually transmitted infections; she needs to be prepared for the emotional consequences of sex as well.

Some teens describe feeling more mature after their first sexual experience; some feel like the whole event was a bit of an anti-climax; and others are caught off guard by how exposed and insecure they feel. Flag this for her and let her know that if she feels sensitive or vulnerable after sex, it's okay, the feeling will pass. Encourage her to practise self-care and let her know that if she wants to talk to you about it afterwards, you promise to be helpful and not ask too many questions.

Your daughter also needs to know that she can say no to sex at any time, even if she's already agreed to a date and time, and even if she's had sex before. An alarming number of teenage girls think agreeing to sex is as good as entering into a legally binding contract. Far too often I hear, 'But I've already told him we can have sex, I can't just back out … can I?' or 'But we've already had sex, isn't it weird if I say no this time?' The idea of saying no is unthinkable, and it shouldn't be. Encourage your teen to think her decision through carefully and only agree to sex if she's ready, but make sure she knows she can change her mind at any time, the week before, the day before, or right in the middle of things if she stops feeling right about her decision. Most teenage girls look at me like I'm crazy when I tell them they can change their mind in the middle of having sex if they don't feel comfortable: 'I can't just *stop* if we've already started having sex.' They're usually shocked by my response:

> Hell yes, you can! If you're not sure, don't sleep with him; wait until you know you're ready. If you think you're ready but realize you're not once your clothes are off, you can absolutely change your mind and say no. Tell him you're sorry, you thought you were ready for this but you're not, and put your clothes back on. If he's a decent guy he'll understand. If he gets mad, he's a jerk, and not someone you want to be sleeping with anyway.

Talk about what being ready actually means

It's good to encourage your teen to wait until she's ready to have sex, but 'ready' is a vague term and she might feel confused about what this means. Identify a few key indicators of readiness and discuss these with her. Here's a few I talk about with teens on a regular basis:

+ You want to have sex because *you* want to have sex, not because you want a guy to like you more and not because other people think you should. If you're having sex for other people, wait.

+ You feel comfortable talking to your boyfriend about sex. If you don't feel comfortable talking about it, you definitely shouldn't be having it.

+ You've thought about how you'll protect yourself against pregnancy and sexually transmitted infections. If your boyfriend doesn't want to wear a condom, tough. It's not worth the risk. The contraceptive pill will guard you against pregnancy, but it won't protect you against sexually transmitted infections. If you're not ready to stand your ground and tell your boyfriend he has to wear a condom, wait.

+ You've talked to your boyfriend about what sort of relationship you both want. If you want a relationship and he's non-committal or he says he wants a relationship but he doesn't make time to see you and he never calls when he says he will, think about whether this is a guy you want to be intimate with.

+ Does the thought of having sex make you feel anxious or uncomfortable? It shouldn't. If it does, wait.

+ If the thought of being naked in front of someone else doesn't feel right, wait. If you're planning to have sex in the dark and partially clothed, this isn't the right solution. Wait a bit longer until you feel more comfortable.

The decision to have sex is huge and there's a lot to talk about. What your daughter needs is a non-judgmental sounding board, someone to help her consider her readiness from all angles so she can make a well-informed decision she feels good about. Your daughter's friends are as inexperienced as she is, so when it comes to sex she needs that person to be you. Help her to feel comfortable talking to you about sex; respect her privacy, be neutral and ask open-ended questions to get her thinking. Don't try to cover everything in one conversation because you can't; sex is an ongoing conversation, not one you can tick off your parental to-do list. Look for opportunities to talk to her about sex and if none arise naturally, start the conversation anyway.

What if my teen doesn't open up?

Even if you nail your approach, your teen might use monosyllabic responses to boycott conversations about sex. Don't panic. Some teens are talkers, some aren't. Don't let her lack of interest deter you, but don't persist with a long-winded, one-sided conversation either. Remember, your objective is to make conversations about sex as comfortable as possible so your daughter feels able come to you for advice when she needs to. Forcing a conversation and talking at her won't help you achieve this.

Approach her reluctance to talk to you about sex the same way you would any other fear. Break it down and help her face her fear gradually. When the situation arises, casually ask general, open-ended questions about sex. If she seems responsive, keep talking; if she doesn't, pause the conversation and try again later. Short bursts of conversation like this will help your daughter learn to talk openly about sex without feeling awkward and uncomfortable. As an added bonus, it will help *you* to feel less apprehensive about raising the topic of sex with her as well.

Talking to your teen about sex will be an ongoing conversation that expands and unfolds as your daughter matures. If you make a mess of your first attempt, cut yourself some slack, then dust yourself off and try

119

again. If your second and third attempts aren't much better, take comfort in the fact that sex is a conversation *all* parents mess up, even the 'expert' parents who like everyone to think they have it all figured out. Ignore your daughter's eye rolls and keep at it. It'll get easier.

The power of dads

Daughters look up to their dads. Mums have a hard time getting daughters to sit up and take notice, but Dad, when you talk, she listens. Use this. Don't opt out of conversations about sex — put your discomfort aside and step up. You don't have to talk to her about birth control or the act of sex itself, but you do need to talk to her about sex and her relationships. Make sure she knows that she should have sex when *she's* ready to have sex, not when her boyfriend's ready, not because her friends are doing it, and not because the guy she likes is asking her to. Help her to see that any guy who pressures her to have sex is a jerk, period, and prepare her for the fact that sex won't make guys she likes like her back.

You don't need to sit her down for deep and meaningful dad chats, but you do need to weigh in on the conversation. Your opinion matters to her. Use your dad power to help her make decisions she'll feel good about.

Boyfriends and bedrooms

When your daughter starts bringing boys home it's a game changer. You'll feel like she's four years old again and can't be left alone, and your parenting instincts will be on high alert. Fear will make you want to impose a blanket 'no boys in the house' rule, but in the interests of keeping your friends close and your enemies closer, do the opposite. If your daughter gets a boyfriend, invite him to dinner, have him over at the weekends, get to know him.

It's not unreasonable to set ground rules — especially where bedrooms are concerned — but involve your daughter in the process. Discuss your concerns and preferences, listen to her thoughts and opinions, and try to reach a mutually agreeable solution. Her level of maturity and reasonableness might surprise you, and she's far more likely to respect your requests if she feels you've made an effort to respect *her* point of view. For effectiveness' sake, be open to negotiation.

How much privacy you're willing to give your daughter and her boyfriend will depend on your personal beliefs and the level of trust you have in her, but there are a few things worth keeping in mind while you negotiate. First, it's fairly typical for teens to have platonic friendships with members of the opposite sex. A male friend doesn't necessarily mean sex is on the horizon. Second, your daughter can have a boyfriend and not be sexually active — one doesn't guarantee the other. Finally, no teen wants to have sex while their parents are in the next room. The thought of suspicious sounds coming from her bedroom might make you want to take her door off its hinges, but most teens really only want privacy for privacy's sake. It's not always about sex.

Bedroom ground rules

Your main concern will be your daughter having sex under your roof, and hers will be privacy. These concerns might seem at odds with one another, but it is possible to reach a mutually agreeable solution. The ground rules you set will differ depending on your daughter's age, and the beliefs and values of your family, but example guidelines are listed for you below:

+ All parties agree that an adult must be home when boyfriend visits.
+ All parties agree that the bedroom door must be left slightly ajar when boyfriend visits.
+ All parties agree that when boyfriend visits, at least some time must be spent outside the bedroom interacting with the rest of the family.
+ All parties agree that Mum/Dad will knock before entering the bedroom.
+ All parties agree that Mum/Dad may enter the bedroom at any time (knocking first) and will do so at regular intervals.

The important bits

+ Your daughter's decision to have sex is hers; it's not a decision you can control. She can have sex whether you want her to or not.
+ Most teens aren't sexually active, but that's not reason enough to avoid talking with your daughter about sex.
+ Sex is an awkward topic of conversation, but your daughter needs your help to make a considered decision she'll feel good about.
+ Talking about sex isn't a one-off conversation you can tick off your parental to-do list. Talk about sex regularly, in short bursts.
+ DON'T put your teen on the spot and demand to know if she's sexually active.
+ DO use open ended, indirect questions to start a conversation about sex.
+ DO stay neutral and DON'T be a judgmental listener, or she won't come to you for help when she needs it.

+ DON'T just talk to your daughter about sexually transmitted infections and pregnancy; help to prepare her for the emotional consequences of sex as well.
+ DO empower your daughter to say no and talk to her about what being ready means.
+ DO set limits around bedroom access, but negotiate and involve your daughter in the limit-setting process.

10

WHEN YOUR DAUGHTER'S THE QUEEN OF DODGING RESPONSIBILITY

Your daughter will develop a number of new skills over the course of her teenage years, but early on she'll display a special talent for dodging responsibility. When the dishwasher needs unpacking she'll be noticeably absent; when she's penalized for handing an assignment in late, she'll blame her teachers for mismanaging her assessment load; and when she fails to be home by curfew she'll blame her friends for misreading the bus schedule or the Uber driver for running late. Her endless excuses and the speed with which she deflects blame will be tiresome, and you'll wonder how much more you can take, but you have more control than you think over your daughter's attitude towards responsibility.

Your teen's inability to accept responsibility can be a passing phase or a more permanent problem — it all depends on the lessons she learns from you. It might be hard to accept, but while immaturity is partly to blame for her responsibility dodging, the truth is, most teens learn to dodge responsibility because their parents give them a free pass.

Up till now, you've taken responsibility for your daughter's needs because she needed you to. As an infant, you made sure she was loved, clean, well rested and nourished because she wasn't able to do these things for herself. When she started school, you made sure she was up, dressed, fed and out the door on time in the mornings, because if left to her own devices she wouldn't have been. You've been responsible for helping her to get school projects in on time, and for making sure she has everything she needs — clean clothes, meals, sleep, food, play dates, lifts to after school activities, and then some. Everything you've done, you've done for her because she needed you to. She hasn't had the skills she's needed to be responsible for herself, but what about now? As a teenager, does your daughter still need you to take responsibility for her or is this a habit you need to break?

At some point, your daughter will leave home and be responsible for her own deadlines, her own self-care and her own life. Even before this, she'll be responsible for major life decisions, like which subjects to pick in senior school, when to start having sex, and whether or not to experiment with drugs when her peers are. How well she takes to these responsibilities will depend on the lessons she learns now. Your daughter may have needed you to be responsible for her in the past, but she's entered adolescence and her needs have changed; what she needs from you now is help to learn the ins and outs of accepting responsibility.

Are you giving your daughter a free pass?

Be honest, how many times have you asked your teen to stack her plates in the dishwasher, but cleaned up after her when you've found a pile of dirty dishes on her bedroom floor? How many times have you suggested she start her assignments ahead of time to avoid the panic attack that leaving things to the last minute inevitably triggers, only to stay up late and help her finish a major work the night before it's due? And how many times have you spoken to her about her phone limit, threatened to take her phone away, but paid, on her behalf, the excess usage charges she's accrued?

There's a huge difference between giving your teen responsibility and making her accountable. Take her laundry, for example. If you give your daughter the responsibility of putting her clothes in the dirty clothes basket, but wash her clothes anyway when you find them strewn across the bathroom floor, you inadvertently take this responsibility back from her. She hasn't been held accountable for the task you gave her because you've given her a free pass. It doesn't matter if you lecture her later and emphatically remind her that you're not her personal maid, your actions send a clear message: her clothes are your responsibility. Why else would you wash them when they weren't where they were supposed to be?

It doesn't matter how clearly you communicate your expectations; words alone won't teach your daughter to be responsible. To learn personal responsibility your daughter needs to be held accountable for her choices.

What teaching personal responsibility looks like

Holding your daughter accountable means not intervening when she makes a poor choice and giving her the opportunity to learn from natural consequences, like having no clean clothes to wear because the dirty ones didn't make it to the laundry for washing, they were left on the bathroom floor instead. You can transfer her dirty clothes from the bathroom to her bedroom if you can't stand to look at them, but if they're not left in the right place, don't wash them. Yes, you'll have to endure a Category 5 meltdown when she realizes the top she wants to wear is dirty, but it's worth weathering the storm. Her top is dirty because she neglected her responsibility and chose to leave it on the bathroom floor. That she can't wear it now when she wants to is frustrating, but it's this frustration that will draw her attention to the need to make a better choice next time.

The cost of colluding with responsibility dodging

Your daughter's instincts will guide her to dodge responsibility and she needs your help to break this habit. Giving her responsibility but taking this responsibility back when she comes face to face with consequences she doesn't like might help to avoid massive meltdowns in the short-term, but it's a band-aid solution and one that robs her of the opportunity to learn to be accountable for her mistakes. Over time, continuing to take on your daughter's responsibilities as your own can affect her confidence as well. It deprives her of the chance to see that she's capable of coping independently, and this can make her transition to adulthood a bumpy one.

Consider the case of Zoe. At seventeen years old, Zoe is in her final year at school. In the past, Zoe and her parents have gotten along well, though there's been a change in Zoe's attitude in the last few years and her parents have reached breaking point:

> She expects us to drive her places and pay her way when she goes out with friends, but god forbid we should ask her to do anything around the house. I have to nag her so much to unpack the dishwasher, it ends up being easier if I just do it myself. She leaves her things all over

the house and never picks up after herself, she just waits for us to do it for her. I think she thinks I'm her personal maid, chef and chauffeur!

She started a new job recently and we were really pleased because we thought a job would help her to be more responsible, but she's so disorganized! I'm lucky if I get five minutes' notice that she needs a lift to work, and if she's late or her uniform isn't clean, somehow it's my fault. I'm so sick of all the fighting. I don't wait for her to tell me when she's working any more; her work emails me her roster directly and I forward it on to her. At least that way I'm never caught off guard. I feel so bad for them. She's missed two shifts already because she wanted to go to the movies with her friends instead. She didn't bother telling her work — she just didn't show up. When they phoned I had to lie for her and tell them she had gastro. I confronted her when she got home, but we got into a huge fight because she couldn't see what the big deal was!

We love her, we really do, but we're struggling to like her much at the moment. She's just so hard to live with.

Zoe's parents have every right to feel frustrated; Zoe is being a spectacular pain in the butt. However, to be fair, part of the problem is that the line of responsibility between Zoe and her parents is blurred. Her parents have given her responsibilities — picking up after herself, unpacking the dishwasher, letting them know in advance when she needs a lift to work — but to avoid arguments they've inadvertently taken these responsibilities back from her. Taking over responsibility for her work roster might help Zoe's parents to know her work shifts in advance, but it's a band-aid solution and it doesn't teach Zoe to be accountable for her lack of planning. Covering for Zoe when she doesn't show up at work also doesn't do her any favours. It might stop her from getting fired in the short-term, but it teaches her that neglecting her responsibilities is relatively harmless.

If Zoe's parents want Zoe to be responsible, they need to hold her accountable for her responsibilities. This means not giving her money unless she contributes to chores around the house, refusing to give her a lift to work if she hasn't given enough notice, and not covering for her if she skips work to hang out with friends. If she gets in trouble at work because she's late or doesn't show up for her shift, so be it. A roasting from her boss is a direct consequence of her choices. If she can't do what her friends are doing because she can't afford to, too bad. She had plenty of opportunities to earn money but chose to skip work and shirk her responsibilities around the house. Zoe's parents will find it hard to watch Zoe face the consequences of her decisions; she'll be upset and angry and she'll make her feelings known. But as hard as it'll be for them to watch her be upset, as they're starting to see, living with a teen who dodges responsibility is harder.

It might seem easier to step in and take over when your daughter's failing to fulfil her responsibilities, but it's a trap. The harder you work and the more responsibility you take on on her behalf, the less motivated she'll be to step up and take on any responsibility herself. Personal responsibility is a hard lesson to learn, but if your daughter's going to grow to be a competent, reliable and self-sufficient adult, it's a necessary one. Don't collude with her responsibility dodging; make her accountable and teach her to own her responsibilities instead.

Lay the groundwork for personal responsibility

Teaching personal responsibility means giving your daughter responsibilities and resisting the urge to step in and take over when the wheels start to fall off. If your teen is relatively immature and you're worried about her ability to take charge, make the transition a gradual one. Work on one or two areas of responsibility to start with, and when you see her learning from her mistakes, take this as a sign that she's ready for more responsibility in other areas as well.

Before you start, make sure you explain in full the changes you're planning to implement. Be as clear and specific as possible, and outline exactly what will be different moving forward. Remember, you're changing the rules and this is all new to your teen; if she doesn't know exactly what's expected of her, she can't make the transition with you. If you've chosen to work on school work first, let her know that you've given it some thought and you think it would be best if she took responsibility for keeping track of her due dates from now on. So that she clearly understands what this means, spell out for her that even though you've helped her with her assignments in the past and given her reminders, you think it's best if she takes full responsibility for her assignments and you don't get involved.

If you want to target her being responsible for getting herself up and ready in the mornings, be just as clear with her about what this means. Explain that you're not going to drag her out of bed any more, even if she's not up on time, and that if she's not ready by the time you need to leave, she'll need to find her own way to school.

Teaching personal responsibility

The areas of personal responsibility you target will depend on where your daughter falls short, but common problem areas you might want to look at are listed for you below.

Money: If your teen thinks money grows on trees, help her to accept responsibility by giving her an allowance. Her allowance should be for more than just treats and luxury items: make her responsible for things she needs like clothing, lunch, travel costs or phone credit as well. If she spends her allowance without factoring in the necessities, too bad. She'll need to go without until next month. It won't be a mistake she makes twice. If she ends up in debt — for example, if she accrues excess usage charges on her phone — deduct this from her next allowance and/or delay her allowance until her debt is paid off.

School work: If you're in the habit of helping your teen meet homework due dates and assignment deadlines, take a step back and hand this responsibility over to her. If she's open to it, help her set up a school calendar or homework reminder system (see p. 23 for ideas), but then leave the rest up to her. Rest assured, if her homework's not getting done or her assignments are getting handed in late, she'll be pulled up on this at school.

Being organized with time: Your daughter is old enough to get herself out of bed, so if you're still functioning as her alarm clock, stop. Likewise, if you're still laying out her clothes, packing her lunch and helping her manage her time in the mornings, take a load off. These are all jobs she's old enough to do without you. If it means leaving the house with messy hair and a half-packed bag, so be it. You won't be her favourite person for a period, but she'll learn quickly to be better organized with her time.

Chores: Chores are an effective antidote to entitlement. Don't give your daughter a free pass by doing everything for her. If her laundry isn't where it's supposed to be, don't wash it. If you can't see her bedroom floor through the mess, don't vacuum it. It's okay to make chores like bedroom cleanliness a condition of her allowance, but keep some chores separate. Make her responsible for a job that contributes to the family as a whole, whether that be unpacking the dishwasher, vacuuming, cleaning a bathroom or helping a younger sibling with their homework, and don't pay her for her time. Chores are part of being a family and some jobs should just be expected.

Decision-making: In the not-too-distant future your daughter will be responsible for making her own life decisions. Some will be relatively small, like whether to finish an assignment or hang out with her friends, and others will be more significant, like which course to study at university and which career path to take. Good decision-making takes practice, and if she's going to make smart decisions in the future, that practice needs to start now. Let your daughter practise being accountable for her decisions. It may mean sitting back and watching her make a few mistakes, but better now than later.

Let natural consequences run their course

When given the opportunity, your teen might step up and take to personal responsibility like a duck to water. If she makes mistakes but owns these mistakes and learns from them, give her lots of positive feedback and help her to take on more responsibility in other areas as well.

If the transition isn't so smooth and she fails to make responsible choices, resist the urge to step in, and instead let natural consequences do their work. When she's in a panic the night before her assignment is due because she started it too late, empathize with her distress, show her compassion, but don't help her to finish her assignment. She'll have a list of reasons ready for why she's not to blame for her last-minute panic — 'Our teacher has been giving us too much work!' — but don't get drawn into her excuses. Don't write a note excusing her from school, and don't stay up late to help her. In her victim mindset she thinks she's blameless, but the truth is she could have started her assignment earlier or at least asked for help before now. Fact is, she chose not to. If she has to lose marks for handing in an incomplete assignment or handing her assignment in late, that's just the way the cookie crumbles.

If she gets up late and isn't ready for school by the time you need to leave, don't wait for her. Leave her money for a bus and task her with getting herself to school. If she throws a tantrum and skips school because you left without her, don't cover for her. Leave it in the hands of her school, even if it means she'll land a detention for her unsanctioned day off. She won't like it, but she will get up earlier in the future.

Challenging her victim mentality

When your daughter defaults to deflecting blame, don't collude with her excuses. Show compassion for her predicament, but help her to accept that she's at least partly to blame for the situation she's found herself in. Avoid directly blaming her with statements like 'You've got no one to blame but yourself' — this won't get you very far. Instead, ask questions that encourage accountability, like, 'Do you think there's anything you could have done differently to avoid things ending up this way?'

When she tells you she's blameless, that there's nothing she could have done differently, gently challenge this. Point out that she's had her assignment for six weeks, for example, and could have sought help before now, or that she could have made it to school if she'd gotten up earlier as you'd discussed. Brace yourself for fireworks when you do, because she won't like you suggesting she's not the victim she thinks she is, but don't get drawn into an argument; the back and forth will only help her practise her excuses. You've planted the seed and that's enough. Leave her to reflect on this more in her own time.

Hold strong, even while she tantrums

Exposing your daughter to natural consequences almost guarantees a meltdown. If you've been protecting her for quite some time, the meltdowns will be fairly substantial, but don't let that deter you. Intervening and saving her from the consequences of her actions might help to avoid a tantrum in the short-term, but it won't help her build the skills she needs to accept responsibility for her mistakes.

It can be hard to sit back and watch your child suffer through the consequences of her poor decisions. You'll feel conflicted about not intervening and want to step in and solve her problems for her when she's upset; but as backwards as it may seem, *not* intervening is the kinder course of action. You're not always going to be there to save your daughter from her mistakes, and letting her face the natural consequences of her decisions now is what will help her learn to accept responsibility and make better choices in the future. If you feel yourself wavering, take a minute to reflect on these questions before you take action:

+ Is it more important for my teen to avoid distress now or to learn to be responsible for her choices?
+ If my teen gets it wrong this time, what might she learn that will help her to make a better decision next time?
+ If I intervene now, what might I stop her from learning?

Your teen won't get things right the first time round. Personal responsibility is a skill and she's still learning, but give her the opportunity to learn from her mistakes and see what she does next.

When to ditch natural consequences for directive parenting

As important as it is for your teen to learn from the natural consequences of her choices, there will still be times when you need to revert to your old parenting approach and be more directive. But be careful to only switch to directive parenting when there's a *need* for this, not just because you'd prefer to intervene to avoid a meltdown.

As a general rule, only ditch natural consequences when there's a risk to your teen's safety or when not intervening has the potential to have an irreparable effect on her future. For example, if you suspect your daughter is experimenting with drugs or engaging in other risky behaviours like coming home after curfew, don't rely on natural consequences — implement parent-imposed consequences instead. Similarly, if your teen is staying on her phone all night and is perpetually sleep deprived, or if there's a steep decline in her academic performance, these are indicators that she isn't ready for the responsibilities she's been given and needs you to step in and be more directive in your parenting approach.

Practise what you preach

An alarming number of adults are as bad as teens at accepting responsibility. The frivolous lawsuits that often make the news are particularly good examples of this. Take, for instance, the man who sued Starbucks when he spilled hot coffee on himself. He wanted Starbucks to be held accountable for his burns and thought suing was the right thing to do. The judge and jury disagreed.[1] Or the woman who sued Google for damages after getting hit by a car while using Google Maps. The app had instructed her to walk across a busy highway with no pedestrian walkways, which is how she ended up injured.[2] Apparently, she trusted Google Maps more than her own commonsense.

Frivolous lawsuits might be an extreme example, but adults dodge responsibility on a daily basis and it's a problem because so much of what your daughter learns will come from what you do, not what you say. If you want her to accept responsibility, *you* need to resist the urge to blame others as well. When you're late because you didn't leave the office on time, own it, don't blame the traffic. When you're fined for overstaying your limit in a parking bay, don't blame the ranger for giving you a ticket, accept responsibility. When you're on your phone more than you should be at home, acknowledge your fault, don't blame work. And when you're like a bear with a sore head, snapping at everyone you live with, apologize, don't use work stress to justify poor behaviour.

The long and short of it is this: when you deflect blame, you model the behaviour you want your daughter to stop. Practise accepting responsibility in your daily life and let your actions be her teacher.

The important bits

+ For the first part of her life, you've taken on your daughter's responsibilities as your own. An important part of her development is learning to be responsible for herself.
+ Giving responsibility is different from holding your daughter accountable for her responsibilities.
+ DO set clear expectations so your daughter knows exactly what she's responsible for.
+ DON'T step in to save your daughter when she makes poor decisions; hold her accountable and let her learn from the natural consequences of her choices.
+ DO help her to accept responsibility for her actions by using strategic questions to poke holes in her 'I'm the victim' narrative.
+ DON'T collude with her excuses and attempts to dodge responsibility.
+ DO be a good role model and practise accepting responsibility in your own life as well.

11

WHEN YOUR DAUGHTER WANTS TO USE SOCIAL MEDIA

Parenting is no easy task. There are so many rules and expectations, getting it 'right' is nearly impossible, and that's just real-world parenting. When your daughter's old enough to start using social media, it adds another dimension. Suddenly you're responsible for guiding not only her real-world behaviour but her online presence as well, across *multiple* social media platforms — Facebook, Instagram and Snapchat, to name a few.

Most teens are active on social media. According to the Pew Research Center in the United States, a large majority of teens — roughly three in four — use social media, 70 per cent are active on multiple social media sites, and 40 per cent check their social media 'several times a day'.[1,2] And girls are the worst offenders. A recent survey by Common Sense Media — also in the United States — found that girls are more likely to use social media on a daily basis and they're also more likely to spend more time each day on social media, roughly 2.5 hours daily compared to the 1.5 hours boys spend each day on social media sites.[3]

Worldwide, findings are pretty consistent. Around 80 per cent of teens surveyed by the Australian Psychological Society, for example, admitted to connecting to social media at least once per day, and over half said they checked social media five or more times per day. Twenty-five per cent of teens admitted to 'constant' social media use, 53 per cent admitted to using social media in the fifteen minutes before bed, and 37 per cent said they used social media in the first fifteen minutes after waking.[4] It's perhaps no surprise then, that like teens in the United States, teens in Australia spend an average of 2.5 hours each day on social media. That's nearly twenty hours a week. Almost one full day.

If your daughter has a pulse, social media is going to spark her interest. With everything that's been written about cyberbullying and the negative impact of social media on self-esteem, you might feel compelled to ban Facebook and Instagram all together, but the truth is, if your daughter wants to use social media she'll find a way to access it, with or without your permission. An all-out ban also cuts her off from the positive aspects of social media — hard to believe I know, but yes, social media use can actually be beneficial for teens — and it also won't help her learn the skills she needs to use social media responsibly.

There are definite downsides to social media, but there are upsides as well, and you don't have to ban your daughter from Facebook and Instagram to keep her safe. With the right scaffolding and a good digital parenting plan you can help her have a positive online experience and at the same time protect her from potential risks.

139

The downsides of social media

There are a number of downsides to social media that can't be ignored. Cyberbullying is one of the most widely recognized downsides, and for good reason. Between 10 and 30 per cent of kids and teens are bullied online each year — and that's just the cases we know about. Bullies use social media to post nasty comments, spread vicious rumours and share humiliating photos, and you only have to watch the news to see the impact of this. Cyberbullied teens are more likely to suffer from anxiety and depression, and far too many teens self-harm or take their own lives to escape their online torment.

Content that encourages eating disorders and negative body image is also widespread. 'Pro-ana' (short for pro-anorexia) and 'pro-mia' (short for pro-bulimia) accounts paint eating disorders in a positive light, and 'thinspiration' accounts — accounts featuring pictures of frighteningly skinny girls with tiny waists and concave stomachs and 'inspirational' quotes like 'When you start to feel weak and dizzy, you're almost there' or 'Your perfect body is within you, buried under a layer of fat' — expose teens to toxic body image messages and unhealthy diet tips. Encouragingly, most social media platforms have made a commitment to ban content that promotes eating disorders, and they've made good on this commitment by disabling offending accounts and prohibiting searches for #thinspiration, #proanorexia and #probulimia; but even with these measures, pro-eating disorder content still exists. It's cleverly disguised amongst health and fitness content and less obvious hashtags like #fitspiration, but it's there, and unless heavy penalties are introduced to discourage individuals from posting eating disordered content, it's unlikely to disappear any time soon.

The comparison-based thinking that social media encourages can negatively affect the self-esteem of teens as well. Teens scrutinize their appearance in photos and negatively compare their own appearance, body shape and weight to that of their friends and everyone else in their social media sphere, and it makes them feel like everyone else is better looking, prettier and skinner than they are. But it's not just appearance comparisons teens get drawn into; social media also encourages life comparisons. Teens forget that what they see in other people's feeds isn't reality, but a carefully edited highlights reel of someone else's life, and they're tricked into thinking they're not as popular or interesting as everyone else in their social media world. They obsessively monitor and compare how their content performs against that of their friends, and when shared posts don't receive the requisite number of Likes, it only adds to their distress. Why? Because for many teens on social media, Likes and Follows aren't insignificant; they're a measure of popularity and self-worth. In the world of teens, you're really only someone if Facebook and Instagram say you are.

It's worthwhile mentioning that the need for teens to be constantly connected to social media is also a problem in its own right. According to the Australian Psychological Society, 63 per cent of teens aged between thirteen and seventeen feel worried or uncomfortable when they can't access their social media accounts and, perhaps unsurprisingly, 60 per cent admit to feeling brain burn-out from their constant connection to social media.[5] This chapter focuses on tips for helping your daughter to have a positive online experience, but for advice on setting limits for how much time your daughter spends on social media see Chapter 5, 'When your daughter won't get off her phone'.

Why should I let my teen use social media?

There are definite risks with social media, but it's not all bad. In fact, there's a growing body of research to suggest that social media can be beneficial for teens. No, really. The results of some studies suggest that because social media provides a platform for relationship building, social connectedness and self-expression, it can actually help to *build* self-esteem in teens. Could teens express themselves in other ways? Probably. Could they feel connected by spending time with friends in the real world? Sure. But teens today choose to connect and express themselves via social media. They post photos on Instagram, share thoughts and opinions in blogs, plan gatherings and catch-ups via Facebook Messenger, and their interest in social media doesn't seem to be getting any less.

There's no clear-cut answer for how social media impacts teens; some studies say social media boosts confidence and self-esteem in teens, others claim it's detrimental. What most studies do seem to agree on is that it's *how* teens use social media that makes the difference. Heavy users, for example, are more likely to be negatively affected, as are teens who use social media more to follow the lives of their friends than to document and share their own life experiences. That's where you come in. By educating your daughter and monitoring her online behaviour, you can help her to use social media in a way that's conducive to her having a positive social media experience.

When should I be worried?

Social media has a number of benefits, but it has its downsides too: cyberbullying, content that promotes eating disorders and self-harm, and edited photos that put pressure on teens to keep up with their fast-paced, more Like-popular peers.

If your daughter sees something upsetting online, she might not tell you about it. If she's being bullied, for example, she might feel embarrassed about what's being said about her, or too hopeless to think reaching out for help will make a difference. Likewise, if she's engaging with content that's eating-disorder related, she'll avoid talking to you about it because she knows you'll disapprove and she won't want to risk you taking away her social media privileges.

Know that your teen probably won't talk to you about any negative experiences she has with social media, and be on the lookout for other warning signs instead. A few common ones are listed for you below:

+ signs of upset, agitation, or nervousness after using social media
+ changes in mood: being more anxious, withdrawn or seeming flatter than usual
+ secrecy around social media use and high levels of resistance to monitoring
+ deleting messages and content to avoid you seeing them
+ obsessive social media use or uncharacteristic avoidance of social media
+ not wanting to go to school or participate in her usual activities
+ withdrawing from friends and family
+ regular headaches or stomach aches (this can be a sign of stress and anxiety)
+ a decline in academic performance
+ changes to sleep, appetite and concentration following social media accounts dedicated to 'healthy living' and 'fitspiration'.

Get to know the social media platforms your daughter uses

One of the first things you should do when your daughter starts talking about social media is create your own social media profiles. Get online and familiarize yourself with the social media platforms she wants to use so you can learn first-hand how each platform works. Having your own profiles will also allow you to connect with your teen on social media so you can monitor her online interactions, at least initially.

There are hundreds of different social media platforms, each with a slightly different focus. Below are a few of the most popular social media platforms, a description of each, and what you need to know to keep your daughter safe. If your daughter's using other apps, make sure you research these too. One thing to note is that while age restrictions might differ across platforms, most platforms have thirteen years as a minimum age of use.

Facebook

Facebook is still the most popular social networking site with teens, and one you're probably familiar with. On Facebook, teens can share photos, links, videos and comments, and by customizing settings they can control the content they see in their feed, who can contact them, and who they share content with. Being able to control content sharing is positive, but be aware that the Facebook Audience Selector Tool also allows teens to share content with a select audience, which you may or may not be part of. This means that even if you're friends with your teen on Facebook, you might not be able to see all of her posts.

Facebook Messenger

Facebook Messenger is an instant messaging app. It was released by Facebook in 2011, but it's separate from the Facebook app described above. Using Facebook Messenger, teens can make calls, send text messages, photos or voice recorded messages to friends or groups of friends. One of the downsides of this app is that it comes with read receipts. Teens can see if someone has read and ignored their messages and this is often a source of conflict.

Instagram

Instagram is a popular photo- and video-sharing app that also allows teens to view, Like and post comments on photos and videos of other users. Photos and videos are shared publicly by default, but privacy settings can be altered to restrict sharing to only the people your daughter has allowed to follow her. Instagram Direct, a private messaging feature on Instagram, also allows teens to share content and comments with individual friends or a small number of friends.

Twitter

On Twitter, teens can 'tweet' short messages to their followers. Users can also follow other people's tweets, retweet the tweets of others, or send direct private messages to other users. Like most other platforms, tweets are shared publicly by default, but can be kept private by using the 'protect my tweets' feature. When tweets are protected, new followers must be approved before they can see any shared content. However, any existing followers will still be able to see and interact with shared content unless they're blocked.

Snapchat

Snapchat is a messaging app that lets users send photos or videos that disappear after they've been seen by the recipient. The seemingly temporary nature of Snapchat has tricked many teens into sending explicit or sexual content they otherwise wouldn't; and while Snapchats might disappear, screen shots can be saved forever. There is a notification feature in Snapchat that alerts senders when a screen shot is taken of their photo or video, but by this time the damage has been done. Tech-savvy teens will also be able to find ways around the notification feature. In terms of security, to avoid receiving unwanted pictures from strangers, users can opt to only receive snaps from people they've accepted as friends.

WhatsApp

WhatsApp is an instant messaging app that uses your teen's Internet connection to allow her to send messages, share content and make calls to her friends or groups of friends for free. The WhatsApp default privacy settings allow any WhatsApp user to see your teen's WhatsApp profile, but you can alter privacy settings to ensure her profile picture and online status is seen only by her contacts.

Tumblr

Users on Tumblr have a blog where they can share text, images, links, quotes and videos. Like re-tweets on Twitter, Tumblr uses can re-blog content shared by other users. Users can make their blogs private, or they can share content publicly but keep certain posts private. One of the downsides of Tumblr is the amount of shared content promoting self-harm and eating disorders.

Create a social media contract

Once you've researched the various social media platforms your daughter wants to use, set up a social media contract. Ask your teen for her thoughts on reasonable guidelines for social media use and use this as a starting point for your negotiations. Negotiate guidelines for her daily usage, her online behaviour, what she will and won't use social media for, and your online monitoring.

The specifics of your contract will differ depending on your daughter's age and the rules of your family, but an example contract I often use with the teens is outlined for you below.

Daily use

+ I will think of social media like TV. I won't use it during homework time, family dinner, when people are trying to talk to me or when I'm supposed to be doing something else.
+ I'll make sure my use is balanced. I'll have one hour of social media-free time each afternoon, and three hours per day of social media-free time on weekends.
+ I know screens before bed can affect my sleep, so I won't use social media in the half hour before bed or any time I'm supposed to be asleep.

Social media use

+ I'll use social media to share my experiences, thoughts and humour with the important people in my life.
+ I'll use social media to express myself and connect with *safe people with similar interests *only* (*friends or friends of friends).
+ I'll let my parents regularly monitor my privacy settings and I'll leave my privacy settings set to the strictest level.
+ I won't use social media to compare my life to other people's because I know social media is a 'highlights reel' of people's lives, not reality. No one posts pictures of themselves sitting at home alone on a Friday night, or crying over a bad mark they were

given on an English assessment. Everyone has parts of their life they don't want to share on social media. *Everyone.*

+ I won't follow people who post about self-harm, disordered eating or dieting, and if other people's posts make me feel bad about myself, I'll block them.

Online behaviour

+ I won't friend or connect with people I don't know.
+ I'll be safe. I won't post information that gives away my address, phone number, school or location. I won't give my passwords to *anyone*, not even my friends.
+ I'll post responsibly. I know that once I've posted something to social media it can end up anywhere, even if I have strict privacy settings, and it can be seen by my friends, friends of friends, friends of friends of friends, family friends, my sports coaches, teachers at my school, future employers, family members, pretty much everyone. I'll think before I post and only post content I'd be happy showing at a family dinner or a school assembly.
+ I know that not posting photos I wouldn't want shown at a family dinner or school assembly means not posting photos of myself semi-naked, even if I'm in a bikini or another outfit that's not as revealing as the picture makes it seem. If I wouldn't want the picture blown up on our mantelpiece, I won't post it.
+ I will interact with people online as I would in real life. I'll treat others with the same amount of respect I would if I were having a face-to-face conversation with them.
+ I won't swear in posts or post sexual comments or nasty remarks, even if they're only meant as a joke. I know that it's easy to misinterpret jokes on social media.

+ I know that screen shots are not my friend. People can capture anything I post online — publicly or privately in a direct message — and share it at a later time. I won't put anything in writing that I wouldn't want shared publicly.

+ I won't post when I'm mad because I know I might end up saying something I'll regret and can't take back. I won't post hurtful, mean or nasty comments; I'll vent to a close friend in person or write in my journal instead.

+ If someone's done something to upset me, I won't address it with them online. I'll make a time to talk to them one-on-one and in person.

+ I won't be a passive bully or encourage bullying by forwarding gossip, hurtful messages or embarrassing photos of other people. If it's something I wouldn't like done to me, I won't do it to others.

+ I won't impersonate other people online by hacking into their account, even if the other person's awful and they deserve it. I'll find another, more constructive way to address my issue with that person instead.

+ If I see something online that makes me uncomfortable, I'll let an adult know so they can help me figure out what to do next.

+ If I receive threatening or unwanted comments, I'll block the user, screen shot the comments and show them to an adult. I know that cyberbullying isn't okay and I don't have to put up with it.

+ If I'm worried about the safety of a friend because they've told me they want to hurt themselves or because they're planning something I think is dangerous, I'll tell an adult immediately, even if my friend has begged me not to. I know it's better for my friend to be angry than unsafe, and safety trumps everything.

Monitoring

+ I know that my parents will regularly monitor my social media accounts to make sure I'm sticking to the terms of this agreement and to keep me safe online. My friends' parents might have different rules and that's okay. Every family is different, but in this family, monitoring is a condition of my social media use.

+ If I want to share content with only a few select friends, that's okay, but I must not block my parents from seeing content on my social media pages.

+ If I break the terms of this agreement, I will have to forfeit my social media privileges for a period of time to be decided by my parents and/or put up with closer parental monitoring of my social media accounts depending on the severity of my breach. I understand that consequences are non-negotiable and that ultimately I'm the one who determines whether or not I have to endure a consequence.

Monitor your daughter's online behaviour

Once you've set up your social media guidelines, you'll need to negotiate a plan for monitoring. How closely you monitor your daughter's online interactions and the people she follows will depend on her age and maturity. You know your daughter best, so you're the best person to judge this, but as a general rule, if your daughter's pretty responsible and has the ability to think before she acts, she probably doesn't need you to monitor her online behaviour that frequently. Following her online and checking her posts every few weeks will likely be enough. If on the other hand she's impulsive or has a history of friendship problems, disordered eating or depression, these are signs she needs you to monitor her online interactions more closely.

Your daughter won't be thrilled about you monitoring her social media. She'll resent being treated like a child and hate having her privacy violated, but she'll also be worried about *your* online behaviour and how this might affect her reputation. Communicating with your daughter or her friends on social media is the equivalent of you showing up at a party expecting to be included. It's embarrassing and, socially, it puts a huge target on her back. She'll need reassurance from you that you won't embarrass her on social media, and the best way to do this is to set up your own contract for monitoring. Ask for her input with this as well, and use your agreed monitoring dos and don'ts to show her that you respect her point of view and take her concerns seriously.

An agreement like the one below will help your daughter to feel more comfortable with your plan to monitor her social media interactions, though, granted, she still won't be entirely happy about it. Stand your ground. Just as in the real world, too much freedom too soon on social media can be a recipe for disaster.

Social media parent monitoring agreement

+ I promise to never communicate with you on social media. I will not Like, comment on or share your photos, and I won't post content to your feed.
+ I promise to never mention posts made by your friends and I will not contact your friends via social media.
+ I will be a quiet observer, not an active one, unless one of your friends is in danger; then I may need to take action because safety trumps everything. If I ever have concerns, I will speak to you first before proceeding with my plan of action.

Monitor, but don't over-monitor or monitor in secret

Too little supervision on social media can be problematic, but so can too much. If you check your daughter's social media accounts too regularly or use her passwords to read her private messages in secret, it will have a hugely detrimental effect on your relationship. Not only that, but because you've violated her privacy you'll make it hard for her to be open and honest with you about her online use. In retaliation she can delete any public or private messages she doesn't want you to see, or she might even surreptitiously set up a new account in a different name that you don't have access to.

Monitoring your daughter's behaviour on social media is important, but over-monitoring or secret monitoring can have adverse consequences. Make sure you have the right balance and lead by example. If you expect your daughter to be honest with you about her online use, be honest with her about your monitoring.

What to do when your daughter breaches her contract

If you catch your teen misusing her social media privileges, address it. Sit down with her and go through your concerns, being as specific as possible. If she's posted an inappropriate picture, explain why it's inappropriate; if you're concerned about some of the people she's following online, help her to understand your concerns; and if her 'funny' comments have gotten her in trouble with her friends, help her to have a better understanding of the role of tone and facial expressions in communication, and the mishaps that can happen online when these cues are missing.

Intentionally or otherwise, if your daughter breaches her social media contract, follow through with appropriate consequences. Exactly what consequence you enforce will depend on the severity of the breach and your daughter's history on social media, but asking her to block any accounts you're not happy about, withdrawing her social media privileges (24–48 hours for smaller breaches, or longer blocks of time for larger breaches), and/or a short-term increase in parental monitoring should motivate your daughter to make a better choice next time. If her actions have negatively affected someone else, she needs to be held accountable for this; withdraw her privileges, increase the frequency of your monitoring and make sure she knows that she'll need to apologize sincerely to the person she's wronged before she can have her social media privileges back.

When your daughter's the target of negative online behaviour

If your daughter's the victim of negative online behaviour, think before you act. Anger will make you want to intervene on her behalf, but this isn't always the best approach. Taking over and fighting her battles for her can make her feel as if you think she's not capable or able to cope with the situation herself, and if you're too reactive your intervention can create additional social problems for her as well.

Take Kimberley, for example. Kimberley's just turned fifteen and for the most part has a good group of friends at school. In the last twelve months she's had issues with another girl in her group — Amanda — and things came to a head recently when Amanda posted some nasty comments on Kimberley's Facebook page. Kimberley's parents monitor her social media intermittently but didn't see the comments — they were deleted before they had a chance — but Kimberley confided in her mum one evening when she was upset. Kimberley's mother was furious, and in a moment of anger contacted other parents at the school to alert them to Amanda's behaviour.

> This issue with Amanda has been going on for way too long and this was the last straw. She's a real little so and so. Kimberley's been nothing but nice to her — it was Kimberley who invited her to sit with them when Amanda was new to the school and didn't know anyone! I just don't think it's right. And, of course, the school wants nothing to do with it — I've tried contacting them already — and neither do Amanda's parents, who won't return my calls; so I contacted the other parents in the group just so they're aware of what's going on.

What Kimberley's mum doesn't know is that she's creating more problems for Kimberley than she's solving.

> I'm so embarrassed. Amanda's comments were mean, but I was handling it and things were getting better, and now Mum's gone and made everything worse. She's acting like a complete psycho! She called all the other parents *and* the school, and I didn't even know about it until I got to school and everyone was talking about it. Now everyone thinks I'm a drama queen and that I'm the one being a cow! Our whole group is split and I've been uninvited to a party because people are siding with Amanda. None of this would have happened if Mum had stayed out of it. I never should have gone to her for help — she's just made everything worse.

Kimberley's mum has the right idea. She's trying to help and wants to show Kimberley she's on her side, but her approach is actually incredibly *un*helpful. Well intentioned as they may be, her actions have added to the conflict in Kimberley's group and Kimberley regrets ever involving her in the first place.

If your daughter is upset about an interaction she's had online, ask her to tell you more about what's been happening. Don't interject with a barrage of questions; listen to what she's saying and just let her talk. While you listen, stay calm. If you over-react or fly off the handle, she's not going to come to you for help in the future, even if she really needs to.

Once you understand the situation, try to be guided by what your daughter needs, not by what your anger's making you want to do, and not by what you would need if you were in her situation. You might seek out practical help when you're upset or stressed, but practical help might not be what your daughter wants or needs. Alternatively, talking it through might be your go-to means of coping, but your daughter might need time to process things herself before she's ready to talk. She definitely doesn't need you taking action on her behalf without talking to her first.

Don't make assumptions about what your daughter needs from you, ask. Offer to be a sounding board if she needs to talk, a distraction if she needs to take her mind off things for a while, or a problem-solving machine if she needs help to come up with a plan of action. Your daughter will appreciate your support so much more if it's helpful help. Listen to what she's telling you she needs and do that.

How to handle cyberbullying

If your daughter has been experiencing serious cyberbullying, there are a number of things you can do. First and foremost, block the bully from your daughter's social media pages. This will mean the bully isn't able to continue to upset your daughter online. It's also important to document cyberbullying by taking screen shots. You can use this evidence to contact the social media platform and ask them to remove any humiliating pictures or abusive messages. If the material doesn't get removed, or if the cyberbullying continues, you can seek help and support from relevant law enforcement agencies. For more information, visit the Office of the Children's E-Safety Commissioner. It's an Australian site, but their website's worth a visit. It's a great resource for any parent trying to keep their child safe online.

Where can I get more information?

Cyberbullying is a complex issue and help can be hard to find. Where you access help will differ depending on where you live, but a few good resources are listed for you below.

+ In the United States, for more information about preventing and responding to cyberbullying go to www.stopbullying.gov.
+ If you're reading this in Canada, visit www.getcybersafe.gc.ca. It's a comprehensive website targeting cybersafety.
+ In the United Kingdom, try www.saferinternet.org.uk. It's a great website with lots of information about how to keep your child safe online.
+ And if you live in New Zealand, try www.connectsmart.govt.nz or www.netsafe.org.nz is also worth a visit. Netsafe is a not-for-profit organization and offers information and advice about online issues.

You can report cyberbullying to your daughter's school too, but be prepared for the fact that her school might not want to get involved, at least not in any meaningful way. While most schools have an anti-bullying policy, their implementation of this policy can be lax. It's common, for example, for schools to shirk responsibility if cyberbullying within their school community occurs outside school hours or off school grounds.

If you need your daughter's school to be involved, make sure you document the cyberbullying with screen shots. Your daughter's word alone won't be enough; for the school to take action, they need proof. If her school seems reluctant to get involved even with proof, try to stay calm. Yelling at the principal will get you nowhere fast, and you'll make things worse for your daughter. Be assertive and let her school know that you'd like them to act, and you'll contact them within a week to see where things are up to. Knowing you plan to follow up should help spur them into action.

When to *stop* monitoring your daughter's online behaviour

As your teen gets older, she'll want more privacy when it comes to her social media use. Her desperate need for privacy might make you wary, but her request isn't necessarily suspicious. Think of when you have houseguests stay for an extended period of time. Despite how much you love seeing them, you're also ready for them to leave by the end of their stay, for no other reason than because you're simply ready to have your house and privacy back. That's how your daughter feels. As she gets older she's going to want privacy for privacy's sake, nothing more, nothing less.

If your daughter's responsible and sticks to the terms of her social media contract, consider gradually reducing your monitoring in acknowledgement of her positive online behaviour and out of respect for her need for privacy. Let her know that you've been impressed by how well she's managed herself online, and her maturity and level-headedness have made you realize she's ready for more online independence.

If you have complete trust in your teen, you might agree to completely remove yourself from her social media world, or if you have residual concerns, you might discuss a more gradual transition. If you usually check your teen's social media accounts on a weekly basis, for example, you might agree to reduce monitoring to fortnightly, then monthly checks, before agreeing to not monitor her accounts at all. If your daughter's happy for you to continue to follow her on social media anyway, great; if she's not, respect her wishes and relinquish your monitoring duties.

It can be tempting to continue to monitor your daughter's social media for longer than she really needs you to. As she gets older, she'll stop turning to you for advice and support — she'll turn to her friends instead. You'll miss the relationship you used to have, and while it's not quite the same, her social media pages will help you to feel connected to her. You're not left in the dark wondering what she's doing, who's important to her, and what her current interests are, because it's all there for you in her social media posts. But once your teen is old enough, and she's proven she can be responsible, the question becomes this: are you monitoring your daughter's online behaviour because she needs you to or to meet your own need to continue to feel connected to her life?

Ongoing monitoring might seem harmless, but if your monitoring is more about your needs than hers, it can start to cause friction in your relationship. More than anything, your teen wants you to trust her. From her point of view, if she's always done the right thing and never given you a reason not to trust her, monitoring past the point of necessity is insulting. Put yourself in her shoes. Imagine working for a boss who insists on micro-managing everything you do, even though your work is always exceptional and you've never missed a deadline. You might be able to initially cut your boss some slack while she gets to know you, but once you've shown her you can work independently and she's seen the quality of your work first-hand, her micro-management will start to frustrate you, and for good reason. It's no different for your teen. If you continue to monitor her social media use when she's proven time and time again that she can use social media responsibly, she'll start to get frustrated. She'll feel as if you don't trust her or think you're trying to control her and she'll start to resent you for it.

When it comes to your daughter and social media, you know her best and you're the best person to decide what sort of social media scaffolding she needs, but be honest with yourself. Make sure your scaffolding decisions are based on what level of monitoring your daughter *needs*, not what level of involvement you'd *like* to have in her online world. Not monitoring her social media activity might feel uncomfortable at first, especially if you've monitored her online presence for quite some time or if she's had issues with friends on social media in the past, but handing responsibility over to her is an important part of her development. Your daughter will be faced with all kinds of important decisions and dilemmas in the years to come. Letting her practice being responsible for her decisions now — online or otherwise — will help to prepare her for this.

The important bits

+ Social media comes with risks, but it also helps teens to feel connected and provides them with a platform to express themselves.
+ It's *how* teens use it that determines whether social media has a positive or negative effect on their self-esteem.
+ DO get online and familiarize yourself with the social media platforms your daughter wants to use.
+ DO create a comprehensive social media contract with clear expectations for online behaviour.

+ DO monitor your daughter's online interactions and who she follows, at least initially, but openly and honestly. Once she's shown you she can act responsibly on social media, DO consider relinquishing your monitoring duties out of respect for her need for privacy.

+ DON'T contact your daughter's friends online or try to communicate with her over social media. You'll embarrass her and inadvertently encourage her to hide her social media activity from you.

+ DO enforce consequences if your daughter breaches her social media contract.

+ DO talk to your daughter about any issues she has online before you take action, and document cyberbullying with screen shots.

12

WHEN YOUR DAUGHTER'S MOODY (AND POSSIBLY DEPRESSED)

Living with a teenage daughter can be like living with a ticking time bomb. One minute she's chatting away happily, laughing about something she's seen on social media, the next she's sullen, angry and withdrawn, barely able to hide the disdain she feels for anyone who has the audacity to enter her room and ask her about her day. Her crappy attitude, sudden mood swings and exaggerated eye rolls make her hard to live with and even harder to like, no matter how many times you count to ten and remind yourself that her hormone-induced bitchiness is an unpleasant but normal part of adolescence.

But while foul moods and an aversion to family interactions can just be a passing phase, they can also be a symptom of something more — depression.

Is depression in teens really a thing?

Moodiness, petulance and voluntary solitary confinement are all hallmark features of adolescence, but teenage depression is a real and prevalent issue, especially in teenage girls. A report on the mental health of Australian children and adolescents released by the Australian government in 2015 showed that nearly 6 per cent of all girls aged between twelve and seventeen have been diagnosed with a major depressive disorder, a figure higher than the 4 per cent of boys affected by depression in their adolescent years.[1]

Internationally, the statistics are even worse. In the United States, it's been estimated that nearly 20 per cent of teenage girls aged between twelve and seventeen have at least one episode of depression each year — that's more than double the rate of depression in boys of the same age. Worse, rates of depression in teens are on the rise. A recent study published in *Pediatrics* found that the risk of teens in the United States being depressed has jumped from 8.7 per cent in 2005 to 11.3 per cent in 2014 and, you guessed it, the largest rate increase has been seen in teenage girls: 13.1 per cent in 2004 to 17.3 per cent in 2014.[2]

Why do some teens develop depression?

The increasing rates of depression in teens raises an interesting question: why? Why are our teens depressed? And why are teenage girls more vulnerable than their male counterparts?

The short answer is there's no one-size-fits-all explanation for why some teens experience depression and others don't, but we do know certain factors make some teens more vulnerable. Teens with depressed parents, for example, are more likely to develop depression, as are teens who are more prone to negative or self-critical thinking.

Teens who're exposed to stressful life events — ongoing peer problems, bullying, family conflict — are also at higher risk. And while it's easy to write off teen stressors as petty (especially when viewed through adult eyes), school stress, body image pressures and friendship issues are all real and valid stressors. Teens don't yet have the hindsight to keep their stressors in perspective, so a poor result on a maths test or a fight with a friend is experienced as intensely as the stress you feel in reaction to pressure to meet unrealistic deadlines at work or conflict within your marriage. Stress is stress, regardless of the cause, and it's helpful to keep this in mind when trying to understand depression in teens.

As for why teenage girls are more likely than teenage boys to develop depression, that's still up for debate. Some researchers argue that teenage boys are less likely to talk about their feelings, making their depression harder to diagnose. Others argue that teenage girls are more prone to depression because they're more exposed to stressors, particularly stressors related to friendship issues and social media.

There's still a lot we don't know about depression in adolescents, but from a treatment point of view the good news is this — we don't necessarily need to know exactly what combination of factors triggered a teen's depression to help them break free of their low mood.

How do I know if my daughter's depressed?

Depression is a term most parents fear, and while it is something to be taken seriously, the word itself is really just a term we use to describe a cluster of symptoms. According to *The Diagnostic and Statistical Manual of Mental Disorders* (or DSM-V — the manual health professionals use to diagnose mental health disorders), to be formally diagnosed with depression, a teen must experience at least five of the following symptoms nearly every day for at least a two-week period:

+ low mood *or* irritable mood most of the day
+ a loss of interest in activities she'd usually show an interest in
+ a loss of pleasure from usually enjoyable activities
+ eating more than usual *or* eating less
+ trouble sleeping *or* sleeping more than usual (including daytime naps)
+ feeling lethargic *or* feeling restless and agitated
+ feeling tired, unenergetic and unmotivated
+ feeling worthless or intensely guilty for no real reason
+ trouble concentrating or trouble making decisions
+ thoughts about death and dying.

What this looks like on a day-to-day basis will differ slightly from teen to teen, but the case of Olivia below is a fairly typical account of the changes parents see when their teen is struggling with depression:

Olivia used to be such a bright, bubbly, happy, outgoing kid. Now she's grumpy all the time and her favourite word is 'no'. She never wants to spend time with us on the weekend, which probably isn't that unusual for a teenager, but she's started avoiding friends on the weekends too, which definitely isn't like her. She's stopped going to yoga on Tuesdays, which is something she used to really love, and it's a battle getting her to netball each week as well. We don't really know what's happened. She's lost her spark. Our biggest problem with Olivia used to be her being too busy and too social;

now she doesn't want to do anything, and trying to get her out of the house is nearly impossible.

And the arguments! She's so argumentative all of a sudden — she never used to be. And we're probably not handling it all that well because we're not used to her being like this. We were patient and understanding initially, but that ship has sailed. Her attitude is terrible and it's really getting under our skin. I took her phone off her last week, which she wasn't too happy about. She'd been moping around the house all day making everyone tense and on edge. When she started throwing a tantrum about having to unpack the groceries it was the last straw. I lost my temper and told her I was sick of her attitude and confiscated her phone for a month. It wasn't my finest parenting moment — I really had a go at her about her negativity, and I think I even told her that we're sick of her — and she's been cold towards me ever since. Later, I tried to apologize for what I'd said but she didn't want to listen, and to be honest, her reaction to my apology reminded me why I lost my temper in the first place.

Her teachers have noticed a change in her, too. She's always been a good student — not top ten in the year good, but average to above average good — but her grades have slipped a bit recently and her teachers have told us she's been handing homework in late and she's missed a few assignment deadlines as well. We honestly don't care about her grades, and we told her that, it's just that the feedback from her teachers made us realize that the problem might be bigger than we first thought.

We thought her moodiness was just her hormones going a bit nuts, but now we're wondering if there's more to it than that.

Teenage depression: know what to look for

The DSM-V diagnostic criteria were outlined for you on pp. 163–4, but also be on the lookout for less obvious signs of depression like the ones below:

+ being emotional and teary
+ feeling bored
+ low motivation
+ changes in appearance (e.g. wearing black all the time, not caring about appearance)
+ poorer than normal academic performance
+ not wanting to spend time with family and friends
+ risk-taking without caring about the consequences
+ frequent headaches or stomach aches
+ increased sensitivity to perceived criticism or rejection.

Helping your depressed teen: getting started

If your daughter is depressed there's a fair chance she'll be bad tempered, and your interactions with her will test your patience. Getting her to do anything — school work, chores, time with family — will be a battle, and your empathy tank will start to run low. But as frustrated as you feel (and you have every right to feel that way; depression *is* frustrating and it's turning your daughter into a disagreeable and obnoxious pain in the butt), remember this: as hard as it is for you, it's hard for her, too.

She's acting like a pain because she's miserable. She's so unhappy that she can't think straight, and everything feels impossibly hard. Getting out to do things feels like way too much effort, and because nothing seems to make her happy anyway, she doesn't see the point in trying. Even socializing feels like more hard work than its worth, so she hibernates at home instead, but being at home doesn't feel that great either, because no one seems to understand her and everything ends in an argument. She's confused by her feelings and desperate to feel happy, but she doesn't know how to make that happen, and that just makes everything worse.

Whichever way you look at it, living with a depressed teen is hard work. Offering unconditional love and support is tough when irritability and apathy are at play, but you'll need to find a way to manage your frustration if you're going to help your daughter through this. How you interpret her symptoms is crucial. If you see her lack of motivation and surliness as laziness and teenage angst, you'll find it hard to be empathic and anger will be your default response. But, if you're able to see her angst for what it is — a symptom of depression — empathy will come more easily. That's not to say there won't still be times when her moodiness makes you want to scream, because there will be. It's impossible to be supportive and nurturing 100 per cent of the time, but understanding her symptoms should help to increase your capacity for compassion, making frustrated outbursts at your end the exception rather than the rule.

When her negativity and gloominess is driving you crazy

If your daughter's depressed, expect her to have a gloomy outlook. It might seem as if she's being deliberately difficult and hard to please, but her negativity is actually a symptom of her depression. Her mood is making it hard for her to think clearly, and it's biasing her outlook; it's blinding her to the positives and making negatives her focus.

To feel happier, your daughter needs help to break out of her negative mindset, but there's a right and a wrong way to approach this. If you try to combat your daughter's negativity with facts and logic alone ('That's not true, you do have friends, you were just out with friends last week') or by bringing her negativity to her attention ('I can't believe you're saying that, why are you being so negative?') it won't help. She'll feel criticized and misunderstood, and it'll only keep her stuck. Likewise, if you try to stamp out her negativity with positivity ('What do you mean you're doing terribly at school, you're doing so well!') it'll only make things worse. She'll feel like you're not hearing her and she'll persist with arguing her point to help you better understand her feelings. She'll be so focused on trying to help you see things from her point of view she'll take little if any of what you say on board, no matter how right you are, and she'll end up even more stuck in her glass-half-empty mindset.

What your daughter needs is your empathy and validation. She needs to feel like you understand her so she can stop defending her negativity and be open to a different, less problem-focused way of thinking. That's not to say that you have to agree with her; you don't. Buying into her negativity will only make things worse so it's best not to go there, but you don't have to agree with her to validate her feelings. Validation and agreement are two separate principles and you can achieve one without falling into the trap of the other.

Let's say your teen's mad because she thinks her friends haven't been making an effort to see her. You know that's not true and her friends *have* been trying to spend time with her, but she keeps cancelling on them at the last minute when she doesn't feel like going. Her perception of the situation is completely inaccurate, and it'll be tempting to jump in and correct her, but don't. If you try to combat her negativity with facts too soon, things will go from bad to worse and you risk pushing her into an even more negative mindset.

As counterintuitive as it feels, validation is the key to helping her to see things more clearly, which means really listening to what she's saying and showing her you understand her. She's not really mad, she's upset. She feels crappy and now on top of that, she's feeling left out and forgotten. You can show her you understand her by cutting to the core issue and validating that — 'I'm sorry you're feeling abandoned by your friends. I know you're having a hard time and you probably need them now more than ever.' You haven't agreed with her, you haven't said, 'I've noticed that as well. I can't believe they're being so insensitive and not being more supportive!' But you've shown her that you understand how she's feeling and that's powerful. Your understanding will help her let go of her negativity, freeing her up to focus on solutions rather than problems.

Help her take action

As powerful as validation is, it can't cure depression. To beat her low mood, your daughter needs to take action. Her mood will make her want to withdraw and do fewer of the things she used to enjoy — like spending time with friends — and fewer of the things she needs to do — like homework. But doing less will actually make her feel worse longer-term. If she stops participating in her usual activities, she'll have fewer opportunities to experience pleasure, and her mood will worsen as a result. If she avoids her school work, she'll feel less overwhelmed in the short-term, but worse as the amount of work she has to catch up on builds, and her grades drop in line with her effort. And while friends might be sympathetic to start with, if she stops saying yes to invitations or starts cancelling plans last minute when she decides she doesn't want to go, her friends will tire of her flakiness and stop reaching out, making her feel lonely and even more depressed.

Encourage mood-boosting activities

If she's feeling down, activity isn't something your daughter's going to jump at, but acting against her mood and doing things even (and especially) when she doesn't feel like it, is what will help to turn her mood around. Being active will increase her opportunity for pleasure, reduce the likelihood of her falling behind on her responsibilities, and help to keep her mind off whatever it is she's feeling down about. Without activities to distract her, she'll have unlimited time to dwell on her thoughts, and because she's feeling down most of these thoughts will be negative. Focusing on negative thoughts will make her mood worse, adding to her negativity, and she'll find herself stuck in a downward spiral.

The upshot? When it comes to breaking free of depression, being active is key. Any kind of activity will be helpful, but the following four categories of activity are known for their mood-boosting capabilities:

1. **Pleasant activities**. Her mood might be a barrier to her enjoying much at the moment, but think of activities your teen used to enjoy before she started feeling crappy. These activities are her pleasant activities.
2. **Mastery activities**. Your teen won't necessarily enjoy these activities, but mastery activities will (a) help her to feel like she's achieved something, and (b) help her to avoid feeling worse later. Think along the lines of school work, music practice, tasks related to organization, or cleaning-related activities.
3. **Social activities**. This can be any activity that helps your daughter feel connected to her peers, whether that be spending

WHEN YOUR DAUGHTER'S MOODY

time with friends outside school hours, participating in social sports, talking to friends on the phone or even texting.

4. **Regular exercise**. Some studies show that regular exercise can help to improve mood in people suffering from depression. Any exercise is great, but generally 30 minutes of exercise (walking, running, group sport, yoga) three times per week is recommended.

Depending on how low she feels, your daughter's mood may make it hard for her to have any positive feelings immediately, so don't expect her to feel happy and pleased after she knocks over some school work or spends time doing an activity she used to enjoy. Change will take time and you'll need to think of it like an investment. Her mood may not change immediately, but continuing to participate in activities even when she doesn't feel like it is what will help her mood to improve longer-term.

When your encouragement to be active is met with resistance

Don't be surprised when your daughter doesn't want to do any of the activities you suggest. Remember, her mood is making it hard for her to feel motivated or find pleasure in the things she used to enjoy, so she's not going to be particularly enthusiastic about your plans for her to participate in activities, no matter how mood-boosting they might be. But while avoidance might be her preferred course of action, it's not a course of action that will help. The more she avoids, the worse she'll feel, and the harder it'll be to get things back on track.

To feel better, your teen is going to have to push herself to participate in activities even though she'd rather barricade herself in her room and be left alone. Her desire to withdraw will be strong, so she might need some additional help. One approach is to offer rewards. You might think feeling happier should be a reward in and of itself, but remember she may not feel better straightaway. She might need to persevere with activities for a few weeks before she notices any improvements to her mood, and rewards will help her to do this.

Help her to set two or three mood goals for the week and then negotiate a reward for achieving these goals. Make sure the goals you set are specific and realistic (e.g. I'll go for a 30-minute walk on Tuesday at 4.30 pm) rather than general (e.g. I'll do some exercise this week). If she's feeling really down and having issues with concentration, two hours of homework won't be a realistic goal, but between one and three 30-minute blocks of school work might be. Likewise, if she's finding it hard to be around people, a whole day with a big group of friends will be too much, but a one-on-one coffee with a close friend might be manageable.

Ask your teen for her input with rewards and use this as your starting point for negotiations. There may be suggestions you need to say no to and that's okay, but before you veto all of her ideas, remember you're asking her to do something really challenging. It's going to be hard for her to persevere with her goals when she's feeling so crappy, and the rewards you use will need to be meaningful enough to offset her desire to avoid and withdraw. If you find the opposite to be true, and she can't think of any rewards, don't let that deter you. Make a list of things you know she'd usually be motivated by and use these to get you started.

What to do when rewards don't work

If your daughter's mood won't let her be motivated by rewards, you may need to add consequences to the mix. Yes, consequences are usually used in a disciplinary context, but when used correctly, they can also help to boost motivation. Your daughter needs a reason to choose activity over avoidance, and knowing activity will help her to feel better longer-term probably won't be enough. If rewards aren't powerful enough to help her choose activity either, consequences might be the answer.

Say your daughter is refusing to go to her weekly netball game because she's feeling down and doesn't want to go. Your initial instinct might be to acquiesce to her request because you don't want to upset her further, but this won't help. Staying home might offer some initial relief — because she feels more comfortable knowing she doesn't have to see anyone or do anything — but withdrawing from friends and skipping her normal activities will reduce her exposure to pleasure and keep her stuck in her low mood. It's not what she'll want to do, but going to her netball game, even only a part of it, will help your daughter break free of her depression.

Selling this idea to her will be a challenge. You can encourage her by asking her to think about how she'll feel later that day if she skips netball versus if she goes, and this might help her to see that not going won't help her to feel better later, and may even make her feel worse. If your encouragement works, and she's able to see the pitfalls of her planned avoidance, ask her to help you come up with a plan for getting to netball, even if only for part of the game.

If she's feeling really down, she might argue that there's no guarantee she'll feel better even if she forces herself to go. If she does, try not to get drawn into an argument about this. Tell her she's absolutely right, there's no guarantee going will make her feel better, but you're confident not going isn't the answer either. Gently let her know that whether or not she goes to netball is her choice, but that if she chooses not to go, she'll need to stay home and not go out to dinner with friends tonight as planned, because you're not sure you feel comfortable with her being away from home if her mood is too low for her to participate in her usual activities.

If she makes a good choice and is able to get to netball for part of the game, praise her and let her know that you're proud of her for overcoming her mood and choosing to be active even though she really didn't want to go. If she chooses to avoid, don't get drawn into a fight. Let her stay home, but make sure you follow through with the consequence you set.

Persist with consequences, even when she lays on a guilt trip

If your teen bucks against consequences with guilt trips, try not to give in. It will be hard to persist with consequences when you're met with statements like, 'I can't believe you're not letting me go out tonight; you know seeing my friends is the only thing that makes me happy', but don't let guilt cloud your judgment. Your teen has chosen to avoid activity and not take the steps she needs to help herself, in spite of your support and the reasonable alternatives you've suggested (i.e. attending only part of the game), and ignoring this will only make things worse. If she skipped school because she was too sick to go, but then wanted to go to a party that same night, would you let her? No, and this is no different. When your teen is unmotivated to help herself and is selective in her efforts, consequences are your only option.

Knowing that consequences are necessary won't necessarily make them any easier to enforce. You'll be reluctant to withdraw privileges because there's so little that makes her happy, but try to focus on the bigger picture. Missing a dinner with friends may initially make her feel worse, but it might also be what helps her to make a better choice next time, and one that will ultimately help her to feel better longer-term.

If you do end up needing to use consequences, just make sure you give your teen a clear rationale. She'll need your help to see that you're not using consequences to punish her for her low mood, even though it might feel this way to her; you're using them to try to help her make better choices. If she continues to choose to avoid despite your forced choices, look at the consequences you're using. Consequences only work if they're meaningful so you might need to make some changes at this end.

If things still aren't getting any better, consider other treatment options and possibly medication.

When nothing seems to be working

A lot has been written about the overuse of medication in kids and teens, some of it quite valid, but if medication is raised as an option, keep an open mind. While medication shouldn't be used in isolation or be the first treatment choice, it can be a beneficial adjunct to psychological intervention. Teens struggling with moderate to severe depression can find it hard to learn and practise mood management skills, and a lack of progress can exacerbate their sense of hopelessness. When psychological strategies don't seem to be working, medication can help to shift mood enough to increase the efficacy of treatment, helping things to get back on track. Medication won't be a quick fix and it should always be used in conjunction with psychological treatments, but be open to considering it as an option if it's advised.

When her depression turns into challenging behaviour

You might find your depressed teen is more irritable than usual and more prone to large-scale tantrums and emotional meltdowns. Knowing she's struggling, your instinct might be to ignore her outbursts and give her more leeway than usual, but this probably won't help. Relaxing your usual boundaries to accommodate her mood might feel like the empathic thing to do, but it can backfire. A shift in boundaries can actually make her feel less secure and more out of control, and this can escalate both her distress and her behaviour.

Coming down hard on her won't help much, either. The more you yell, the more misunderstood your teen will feel, and this will have a negative effect on her mood and cause tension in your relationship. Olivia (p. 164) is a good example. Her parents tried to be patient and understanding, but her moodiness pushed them to their limit. When they finally reprimanded her for her attitude, it was a full-scale dressing down and things with Olivia have been worse than ever since.

If your teen's depressed and her behaviour is testing your patience, try not to change your parenting approach too much. Keep your usual boundaries, but change how you enforce them. Take Olivia's reaction to being asked to help with the groceries, for example. She may well have had a bad day, and her low mood is probably making it hard for her to contain her irritability, but that doesn't make her outburst acceptable. At the same time, her reaction's completely out of character. She's usually a pretty compliant kid and she's definitely not usually this painful to be around, so while her parents need to address her behaviour, they also need to take into account the current problems she's having with her mood.

Compassionate boundaries are key when you're parenting a depressed teen. It's an approach that will help you strike the right balance between empathy and discipline, and it's this balance that will help you to be effective. Keeping with the example of Olivia, a compassionate boundary looks like this.

Parent: (*knowing Olivia's behaviour is out of character and being influenced by her mood*) I think it's best if you go and cool off. I'll come in in a while and we'll chat then.

Parent: (*after allowing 10–20 minutes for teen to cool off*) I'm not sure what's going on for you today, but based on what just happened out there I'd say you're having a bad day. Do you want to talk about it?

Teen: No.

Parent: (*drawing on every possible ounce of patience and understanding they possess*) Okay, well if you change your mind I'm here to listen and help you in any way I can. Screaming at me isn't the best way to let me know you're having a hard day, though. I know you need me to be patient, but I find it hard to stay calm when I'm feeling attacked, so we need to figure out a way around that. We don't need to come up with a solution right now, but we do need to figure something out so I want you to think on it for me.

    In the meantime, I am going to ask you to give me your phone for the rest of the night. Before you say anything, I'd usually take your phone for the rest of the week off the back of what just happened, but I'm trying to be fair and reasonable, so you can have it back tomorrow morning. I'm trying to meet you halfway, but I need you to do the same for me. We can chat more about it later.

If you end up having to go down this path with your teen, once a bit more time has passed and everyone has calmed down, start a conversation about alternate ways for her to let you know she's struggling and agree on a method of communication for the future. Keep in mind that most teens, depressed or not, won't want to have lengthy discussions about how they're feeling, so be open to other means of communicating. One idea might be to come up with a rating system: something like 0 = my mood is awful, the worst it's ever been; 5 = my mood is average, I feel flat but okay; and 10 = I feel happy, the best I've ever felt. This way, your teen can let you know how she's feeling with a number and without the need for a long, drawn out conversation. The exact method isn't important, so long as it's effective and works for everyone involved. Ask your teen for her input and start there.

And if you find it hard to enforce consequences when your teen is depressed, remember this: giving her a free pass isn't doing her any favours. Inconsistent boundaries will make things worse, not better, so stick to your usual boundaries but change your approach. It's what's best for her, but you'll feel better for it as well.

The important bits

+ It's easy to mistake teenage depression for adolescent angst, so know what to look for.
+ Depression is a term used to describe a cluster of symptoms; it's not necessarily a lifelong diagnosis.
+ Living with a depressed teen is hard work, but living with depression is hard, too.
+ DON'T try to combat negativity with positivity and logic. Validate your daughter's distress, but DON'T fall into the trap of agreeing with negative thoughts.
+ Low mood will make your daughter want to withdraw and stop participating in her usual activities, but avoidance won't help, and it may even make her feel worse longer-term.
+ DO set specific and realistic mood goals.

+ DO use rewards to help her participate in mood-boosting activities.
+ If rewards don't work, DO use consequences to help motivate your teen to choose activity over avoidance.
+ DON'T give in to guilt trips; stick to the consequences you set.
+ If low mood makes your teen irritable, DON'T ignore challenging behaviour. Be consistent with your parenting approach but use compassionate boundaries to set limits.

13

WHEN YOUR DAUGHTER'S CUTTING (OR SHE KNOWS SOMEONE WHO IS)

As adults, when we're stressed or down in the dumps we take steps to help ourselves feel better. We seek support from family and friends, take time out from technology or head to the gym for a hit of endorphins. Self-harm isn't something that springs to mind. It's not something we equate with coping, and in fact the idea of causing harm to feel better seems completely nonsensical. But for teens it's a different story. If recent reports are anything to go by, self-harm is fast becoming one of their default means of coping.

What is self-harm?

Self-harm refers to any deliberate, self-inflicted behaviour done with the intention of causing pain or injury. It's very different from suicidal behaviour, which refers to any behaviour done with the intention of ending life. Generally, teens who self-harm to inflict pain or injury <u>don't</u> want to end their life; they're using self-harm to cope and to feel better.

Cutting is by far the most common form of self-harm in teens, but self-harm can also refer to:

+ self-inflicted burns
+ self-directed aggression (e.g. self-strangulation, self-directed hitting, pinching)
+ drug and alcohol abuse, including overdosing on prescription or non-prescription drugs
+ risky behaviour (e.g. binge drinking, unprotected sex)
+ binge eating or self-starvation
+ swallowing sharp objects.

In 2015, a report prepared by the Australian government on the mental health of Australian children and adolescents showed that nearly 15 per cent of twelve- to seventeen-year-old girls had self-harmed at some point in their life. Twelve per cent had self-harmed in the last twelve months. Even more alarming, rates of self-harm were even higher amongst older teens: nearly 23 per cent of sixteen- and seventeen-year-old girls admitted to deliberate self-harm, 17 per cent of those in the last twelve months.[1]

Similar figures are being reported worldwide, and the trend seems to be growing. A recent study in the United Kingdom, as quoted in *The Guardian*, showed a marked increase in the number of teens being admitted to hospital for self-harm, particularly teenage girls. Between 2005–6 and 2014–15, the number of teenage girls admitted to hospital for cutting quadrupled, and even more alarming, the number of girls admitted for self-poisoning — teens deliberately taking a medication overdose though not necessarily with the intention of ending their life — also increased by 42 per cent.[2] Other studies have found similar results. Researchers at the University of Manchester, for example, also found a marked increase in the incidence of self-harm in teenage girls. In fact, their results suggest that between 2011 and 2014, self-harm in girls aged between thirteen and sixteen increased by a whopping 68 per cent.[3]

The research paints a pretty consistent picture: more and more teens are turning to self-harm, teenage girls in particular. It's a global problem and one that's slowly gaining more attention, but it's an issue that leaves most parents feeling completely confused and more than a little out of their depth. So how did we get here and why are so many teenage girls so hell bent on hurting themselves?

Why do teens self-harm?

There are a number of reasons why teens turn to self-harm, but for most it's a coping mechanism. As illogical as it sounds, physical pain offers a distraction from intense emotional distress, and this short-term relief helps teens to cope. Take Lisa, for example. She first started cutting about six months ago to cope with stress.

> My parents think I'm doing this for attention but I'm not — I hate that they know. None of my friends at school know about my cutting because I don't talk about it. A couple of my friends cut themselves on their wrists and tell everyone about it — and I mean everyone — but I don't want anyone asking me questions so I only cut myself where I can hide it, like my hips or lower stomach. If Mum hadn't walked in on me in the bathroom by accident, she still wouldn't know about it. I can't believe she thinks I'm doing this for attention — is she serious?
>
> I know cutting is bad and I shouldn't be hurting myself, but it's the one thing that helps me to feel better

when I'm feeling stressed or upset. It takes my mind off things for a while and sort of shocks me out of my stress. That probably sounds dumb, but it's the truth. I don't like that I do it, and I've tried to stop because it makes me feel guilty afterwards, but then something happens that stresses me out and I do it again. I don't want to cut, but I don't want to stop either because cutting helps me to feel better — I wish my parents could understand that.

Seeking relief from overwhelming emotions is generally the most common cause of cutting in teens, but teens also self-harm for other reasons. Some teens use self-harm to communicate that they're not coping and need help, and although less common, other teens hurt themselves because they believe they're inherently bad and deserve to be punished. Some teens experiment with self-harm to fit in with friends, or because they think cutting makes them seem intriguing, edgy or cool; and a small group of teens self-harm (or threaten self-harm) to influence the behaviour of others — though it's worthwhile stressing this is generally the exception rather than the rule. Tegan's parents below are a good example.

I know this makes us sound like terrible parents, but I really do think she's doing this for attention. We feel manipulated. She'll be happy and calm one minute, but as soon as things don't go her way, she starts making threats. We told her she couldn't go to a party last week, and she told us that if we didn't let her go she'd hurt herself. It's ridiculous, but it's not an empty threat. She's cut herself before — once we had to take her to hospital to have her cuts seen to — and she's so stubborn, we're afraid she'd do it again just to teach us a lesson.

We feel so trapped. If she's not happy with something she just threatens to hurt herself and we give in. She's holding us at ransom and the worst part is it's working. She's getting what she wants and calling all the shots. We can't keep going on like this, but we don't know what else to do.

Signs of self-harm: what to look for

There are several different reasons why teens might self-harm, but coping is the most common. Teens find themselves overwhelmed with intense sadness, anxiety or stress, and self-harm offers temporary relief from these feelings.

Few teens are open and honest about their cutting. Most go to great lengths to keep their self-harm a secret by covering cuts with long sleeves or pants, or by only harming the parts of their body they know others won't see (e.g. cutting on the stomach or upper thighs). Some teens are secretive because they're ashamed; others keep their self-harm hidden because they're afraid of how they'll manage once they're found out and forced to stop using cutting to cope.

If you're concerned your daughter might be experimenting with self-harm, watch her carefully and be on the lookout for the following warning signs:

+ unexplained (or poorly explained) cuts, scratches, burn marks or scars
+ blood stains on her bed sheets, towels or clothes
+ a sudden interest in laundry and doing her own washing
+ blood-stained tissues

+ deliberate attempts to cover certain body parts
  (e.g. wearing long sleeves in summer)
+ avoiding activities which expose certain body parts
  (e.g. swimming)
+ sharp objects going missing (e.g. knives, scissors, safety
  pins, razors)
+ finding sharp objects hidden in unusual places
+ medication going missing
+ finding empty pill packets
+ disappearing for long periods of time when distressed
+ secretive or elusive behaviour.

What *not* to do if your daughter is cutting

There are few things as disturbing as finding out your daughter is deliberately hurting herself. That she's been able to hide something as serious as this from you for as long as she has will make you question whether it's safe to leave her unsupervised, but acting on your fear and taking away her freedom isn't the solution. Not letting her out of your sight and banning her from having contact with friends — virtual or otherwise — might help you to feel more in control and less anxious in the short-term, but it will frustrate your teen and escalate her distress, increasing her risk for self-harm.

Bending over backwards to protect her from stress — whether by giving her a free pass when it comes to school attendance, or facilitating extra time with friends at the expense of homework — also won't help. Avoidance might help her to cope in the short-term, but it will make things harder for her longer-term as she falls behind and has to catch up. Relaxing your usual rules and expectations too much can backfire in other ways, as well. It can mean your daughter learns that self-harm, or talk of self-harm, is an effective way for her to dodge her responsibilities, inadvertently increasing rather than reducing her interest in cutting as a means of coping.

Over-reacting to your teen's self-harm isn't helpful, but neither is complacency. If you ignore her cutting or don't take it seriously, she'll feel as if you don't care. Her distress at this will strengthen her urge to hurt herself or, worse, drive her to experiment with more dangerous forms of self-harm to elicit your compassion. Don't fall into the trap of judging the seriousness of her self-harm by the depth of her cuts. Physically, her cuts may be relatively superficial, but the fact that she feels the need to harm herself at all is concerning and something to take seriously.

The right approach: develop a safety plan

If you know your daughter's hurting herself, don't ignore it — talk to her. Let her know you know she's been cutting and you want to be able to help. Don't put her on the spot and badger her with questions, as it'll only make her uncomfortable; instead, make your focus what you can do to support her moving forward.

Your first course of action needs to be a safety plan. Until your daughter's able to keep herself safe, she'll need you to step in and take this responsibility on for her. She won't love the idea of you involving yourself because it threatens her freedom, but don't be deterred. Explain that you're not planning to be more involved than you have to be, and you don't want to make her upset, but you need to make sure she's safe and okay, and that means being more involved, at least for the time being. If she's still distressed, help her to see that your level of involvement is completely within her control. If she's able to keep herself safe, you'll happily take a step back, but if she continues to deliberately hurt herself, you'll need to persist in helping her with her safety, until you're sure she's ready to resume this responsibility for herself.

There are a number of things you can do to keep your daughter safe. Your approach will depend on her level of risk and the severity of her self-harm, but as a general rule, start by asking her to hand in any objects she's been using to hurt herself, and remove her access to sharp objects and medications around the house. If she's at higher risk or seems determined to continue hurting herself, you might need to take additional action, but try to only intervene as much as you need to.

How can I keep my daughter safe?

When you need to intervene to keep your daughter safe, try not to be guided by fear. As best as you can, match your level of intervention to her actual level of risk. Micro-managing your daughter when she doesn't need you to might help you feel more in control in the short-term, but it will also create tension in your relationship and add to her distress.

As a parent, it can be hard to judge how 'at risk' your daughter is, but the following signs usually indicate a need for closer monitoring:

+ high distress
+ high irritability and agitation
+ social withdrawal
+ frequent self-harm
+ self-harm that's more severe.

Try to be as unobtrusive as possible, though of course at the end of the day, safety trumps privacy.

From least to most intrusive, possible monitoring strategies include:

+ asking your daughter to leave her bedroom door open
+ checking on your daughter at regular intervals
+ asking your daughter to stay in areas of the house where others are present
+ searching your daughter's room for sharp objects or medications
+ sitting in the same room as your daughter and not letting her out of your sight
+ asking your daughter to accompany you when you need to leave the house to run errands
+ checking your daughter's body for cuts
+ sleeping on the floor of your daughter's room.

When to step back and stop monitoring

As your daughter demonstrates she's able to keep herself safe — by using other methods of coping, not self-harm — gradually lessen your involvement. If her self-harm was severe enough to warrant continuous monitoring, look at gradually increasing her privacy again by allowing her to spend short blocks of time in her room with her door open. If you've been allowing her to spend time in her room but checking in with her at regular intervals, reduce the frequency of your check-ins, and if it's something you allowed her to do before, work towards her being able to spend time in her room with the door closed.

Fear will make you want to continue to monitor your daughter regardless of her progress, but try to only monitor her on an as-needed basis. Ongoing monitoring might seem harmless, but if you continue to monitor her purely to appease your own anxiety, it will put pressure on your relationship and it might lessen her motivation to work on her cutting.

Address the underlying causes of her self-harm

If monitoring alone doesn't stop your daughter's self-harm, you'll need to look at what's driving her need to cut. She's hurting herself for a reason, and unless you know what that reason is, you won't be able to support her in learning the replacement skills she needs to stop hurting herself. If she's cutting to cope with distress, for example, she'll need help to learn alternate coping skills so she's less dependent on self-harm to manage difficult feelings. Likewise, if she's experimenting with cutting to connect with friends, she'll have a hard time stopping her self-harm unless she learns to value herself and grows confidence in her worth and likeability. Help your daughter learn the skills she needs to stop cutting, and if you're not sure how, support her by helping her to seek professional help.

What to do when your daughter's not cutting but her friends are

The prevalence of self-harm in teens means that even if your daughter's not cutting, she probably knows someone who is. If it's one of her close friends, you'll be tempted to encourage her to put the friendship on hold for a while, but tread carefully. She's not going to cut ties with her friend just because you tell her to — especially when her friend's going through a difficult time — and because you've made it clear you don't think the friendship is a good idea, she won't come to you for help in the future, even if she needs to.

If your goal is to make sure your daughter isn't adversely affected by her friend's problems, switch tactics. The biggest risk is her feeling

189

overly responsible for her friend's wellbeing, so make this your focus. Help her to set boundaries around what she can and can't do to support her friend, and make sure she knows what action she can take if she ever starts to feel overwhelmed and out of her depth.

Encourage your daughter to support her friend by talking to her about her cutting, being a positive distraction — by planning activities to help take her mind off whatever's upsetting her — and offering to help her find a trusted adult to talk to for support. Concern will make your daughter want to do more than this, but it's important that she understands that taking on a bigger role — acting as a crisis counsellor, for example, and being available at all hours of the day and night to listen and offer advice — starts to blur the lines between being a good support and her taking on her friend's problems as her own, the latter of which will cause her to burn out and lessen her capacity for support. To be of any help to her friend, your daughter needs to know her limits and balance care for her friend with care for herself. Help her to understand this so she can get her balance right.

Your daughter also needs to know that if at any point she starts to feel overwhelmed or stressed by her friend's problems, it's okay for her to seek help from a trusted adult, even if her friend hasn't spoken to anyone else about her cutting. She'll feel conflicted about breaking her friend's confidence, especially if she's been sworn to secrecy, but she needs to know that seeking help is the right thing to do. If she's hesitant, ask her to think through all the benefits of speaking to an adult — her friend's parents, the school psychologist, a trusted teacher — about her concerns, and all the reasons why she feels it's a bad idea. Her biggest concern will probably be her friend's reaction, but encourage her to think about what's more important longer-term: her friend being safe and getting the help she needs, or protecting her friendship and staying in her friend's good books.

If your daughter is really against you involving other adults, her distress will make you want to seek help on her behalf, potentially without her knowledge, but consider the pros and cons of this before you act. Your teen has put her trust in you and she's looking to you for help: breaking her trust and speaking to other people behind her back might mean she won't come to you next time. Getting other people involved against her wishes may end up being your only option, but it should be a last resort. Try to convince her of the necessity of involving other people first, by helping her to see the benefits, not just for herself, but for her friend as well, of seeking additional help.

Managing crisis contact from her friends

Even with the right boundaries in place, if your daughter knows someone who's cutting, there's a chance she'll at some point find herself on the receiving end of a crisis call or text. Pre-empt this and make sure your daughter knows she can always come to you for help if her friend threatens self-harm or contacts her for support in a crisis situation. If the situation does arise, let your daughter know that her friend's safety trumps everything and contact her friend's parents so they're aware of what's going on. If you don't have contact details for her parents and there's reason to believe your daughter's friend is at risk, call emergency services. Give them what information you do have, then leave it with them to take the necessary action to keep your daughter's friend safe.

If crisis contact is an ongoing issue, see if you can get hold of the contact details for your daughter's friend's parents, or failing that, pass your details on to the psychologist at her school so they can ask her parents to contact you. Your daughter might feel uncomfortable with this plan at first, but knowing you have an emergency contact and a contingency plan for future crisis calls will help her feel less stressed.

The important bits

+ Self-harm is common enough in teens that if your daughter's not cutting herself, she probably knows someone who is.
+ Teens self-harm for different reasons, but most teens self-harm to cope with intense emotions.
+ DO take your daughter's self-harm seriously regardless of its severity.
+ DON'T react too strongly or relax your usual rules and expectations too drastically in response to self-harm — it might end up making things worse.
+ DO develop a safety plan to keep your daughter safe, but only intervene as much as you need to.
+ DO work towards your daughter resuming responsibility for her own safety once you see signs she's ready for this (e.g. periods with no self-harm).
+ DO address the underlying causes of your daughter's self-harm.
+ If your daughter has friends who are cutting, DO help her to set boundaries so she doesn't take on her friend's problems as her own, and DO have a contingency plan for crisis contact from friends.

A FEW FINAL
THOUGHTS

It's fair to say that all parents are tested by the teenage years, but if you find yourself living with a teenage daughter who's hypersensitive, self-centred and argumentative, adolescence will be a particularly difficult time. Your daughter's crappy attitude and general moodiness will make her a difficult person to live with, and her reactivity and readiness to argue an easy scapegoat for household tensions and disagreements. But as at-fault as she may be, it takes two to tango, and when it comes to conflict, you're part of the equation as well. It's easy to get distracted by all the things your daughter needs to do differently, but the reality is, if things are going to change it's not just your daughter who needs to be different: *you* need to change, too.

The teenage version of your daughter is different from the pre-teen version, which means the parenting strategies you've relied on up to this point are approaching their use-by date. 'Because I said so' might have been enough to garner her compliance in the past, but fast forward to the present and things have changed. She has her own set of opinions, and when it comes to parenting decisions she wants to be part of the process. Her sudden need to have a say might feel like a deliberate affront to your authority, but her push-back isn't being driven by defiance. What she really wants is to be heard, but so do you, and therein lies the problem. You want her to listen and respect the boundaries you set without questioning them first, but she needs to feel like *you're* willing to listen to what *she* thinks and feels before she's able to do this. When you're not willing to listen, neither is she, and that's when things start to come undone. If things are going to improve, there needs to be a truce, but it needs to come from both sides. Your daughter doesn't have the skills she needs to take the high road yet, but you do — use them. Help her to be more flexible and less argumentative by leading by example. Ditch your old parenting strategies and try a new approach.

For effectiveness' sake, and for the sake of your relationship, be open to a more collaborative style of parenting. If you've always defaulted to a 'you'll do as I say because I'm the adult' parenting approach, collaborating with your daughter will feel uncomfortable at first — backwards even — but stick with it. Despite what you think, and as unlikely as it sounds, compromising won't lose you her respect. Showing her you're willing to listen and take her concerns seriously will actually help you *gain* her respect, and things will run more smoothly in your relationship as a result. Think of it this way: who would you be more willing to listen to and respect — a boss who listens to your concerns and takes into consideration what you have to say, or a boss who tells you in no uncertain terms that they don't care what you think, they want it done their way, period? How your teen feels in her relationship with you is no different. Don't be afraid to compromise: if you show her you're willing to meet her halfway it won't undercut your parenting power, it'll strengthen it.

One important caveat, though — a collaborative approach doesn't mean giving in. Consider this. Your daughter wants to go to a friend's gathering, but the event clashes with a family lunch. You recognize the date and cut her off mid-sentence to tell her she can't go because the lunch has been organized for months and she has to go to that instead. She sees red, and the conversation quickly escalates into a fight. After a lengthy argument you relent and reluctantly agree to let her go, which is effective insofar as it puts a stop to your argument, but ineffective in that it teaches her that, when she wants something, she should be relentless and argumentative because it'll help her to get what she wants. Negotiate with your teen, but don't back down and cave in to her demands to end an argument. Giving in might put an end to conflict in the short-term, but it also inadvertently reinforces her argumentativeness, which will make things worse longer-term.

When your daughter enters her teenage years you'll need to start doing things differently when it comes to advice-giving as well. She may have hung on your every word in the past, but those days are long gone. She still respects you and she'll look to you for guidance when she needs it, but she also values her independence and isn't interested in taking on your opinions as her own without thinking for herself. Unsolicited advice, no matter how well intentioned, won't go down well. If you want what you say to carry any weight, you need to change your approach.

Don't talk *at* her; have balanced conversations. Your advice might be exactly what she needs to hear, but your delivery will determine how much of what you say is listened to, and how much is tuned out. Parents are often exasperated when their daughters willingly listen to the advice I give despite it being the exact same advice they've been imparting for months. 'But that's exactly what I said!' is a phrase I hear frequently — and sometimes the advice *is* the same, but the delivery is different, and that's what makes the difference. So when you need to give advice, think before you speak. Ask open-ended questions, listen to understand, and steer clear of long-winded lectures. You have two ears and one mouth — when it comes to conversations with your teen, be guided by that ratio.

Your daughter's teenage years will be hard going at times, but they're not just hard on you; they're hard for her as well. Be sensitive to her struggles, help her learn the skills she needs to be a well-adjusted, competent and considerate human being, and have patience, lots and lots of patience. Her teenage years will end eventually and you'll forget just how trying they were. In the meantime, hang in there — you're doing great.

ENDNOTES

Chapter 1

1.   Dumontheil, I., Apperly, I.A., Blakemore, S-J., 2010, 'Online usage of theory of mind continues to develop in late adolescence', *Developmental Science*, vol. 13, no. 2, pp. 331–8.

Chapter 3

1.   Kenardy, J., Brown, W.J., and Vogt, E., 2001, 'Dieting and health in young Australian women', *European Eating Disorders Review*, vol. 9, no. 4, pp. 242–54.

2.   Neumark-Sztainer, D., Wall, M., Guo, J., Story, M., Haines, J., and Eisenberg, M., 2006, 'Obesity, disordered eating, and eating disorders in a longitudinal study of adolescents: How do dieters fare 5 years later?', *Journal of the American Dietetic Association*, vol. 106, pp. 559–69.

3.   Pietiläinen, K.H., Saarni, S.E., Kaprio, J., and Rissanen, A., 2012, 'Does dieting make you fat? A twin study', *International Journal of Obesity*, vol. 36, pp. 456–64.

Chapter 4

1.   Lawrence, D., Johnson, S., Hafekost, J., Boterhoven De Haan, K., Sawyer, M., Ainley, J., and Zubrick, S.R., 2015, 'The mental health of children and adolescents: Report on the second Australian child and adolescent

survey of mental health and wellbeing', Department of Health, Canberra, retrieved from: https://www.health.gov.au/internet/main/publishing.nsf/Content/9DA8CA21306FE6EDCA257E2700016945/%24File/child2.pdf

2.   Merikangas, K.R., He, J.P., Burstein, M., Swanson, S.A., Avenevoli, S., Cui, L., Georgiades, K., and Swendsen, J., 2010, 'Lifetime prevalence of mental disorders in US adolescents: Results from the National Comorbidity Survey Replication — Adolescent Supplement (NCS-A)', *Journal of the American Academy of Child and Adolescent Psychiatry*, vol. 49, no. 10, pp. 980–9.

Chapter 7

1.   Dove, 'The Dove Global Beauty and Confidence Report', retrieved from: http://www.dove.com/au/stories/about-dove/our-research.html

2.   Becker, A.E., Burwell, R.A., Herzog, D.B., Hamburg, P., and Gilman, S.E., 2002, 'Eating behaviours and attitudes following prolonged exposure to television among ethnic Fijian adolescent girls', *British Journal of Psychiatry*, retrieved from: http://bjp.rcpsych.org/content/180/6/509.long

3.   Field, A.E., Austin, S.B., Striegel-Moore, R., Taylor, C.B., Camargo, C.A., Laird, N., and Colditz, G., 2005, 'Weight concerns and weight control behaviors of adolescents and their mothers', *Archives of Pediatrics and Adolescent Medicine,* retrieved from: https://jamanetwork.com/journals/jamapediatrics/fullarticle/486190

Chapter 9

1.   Guttmacher Institute, 'Adolescent sexual and reproductive health in the United States', retrieved from: https://www.guttmacher.org/fact-sheet/american-teens-sexual-and-reproductive-health

2.   Finer, L.B. and Philbin, J.M., 2014, 'Trends in ages at key reproductive transitions in the United States, 1951–2010', *Women's Health Issues*, vol. 24, no. 3, pp. 271–9, retrieved from: https://www.guttmacher.org/fact-sheet/american-teens-sexual-and-reproductive-health

3.   Martinez, G.M. and Abma, J.C., 2015, 'Sexual activity, contraceptive use, and childbearing of teenagers aged 15–19 in the United States', *NCHS Data Brief*, no. 209, retrieved from: https://www.guttmacher.org/fact-sheet/american-teens-sexual-and-reproductive-health

4.   Martinez, G.M., Copen, C.E. and Abma, J.C., 2011, 'Teenagers in the United States: Sexual activity, contraceptive use, and childbearing, 2006–2010 National Survey of Family Growth', *Vital and Health Statistics*, vol. 23, no. 31: retrieved from: https://www.guttmacher.org/fact-sheet/american-teens-sexual-and-reproductive-health

5.   Mitchell, A., Patrick, K., Heywood, W., Blackman, P., and Pitts, M., 2014, '5th National Survey of Australian Secondary Students and Sexual Health 2013', (ARCSHS Monograph Series No. 97), Australian Research Centre in Sex, Health and Society, La Trobe University, Melbourne, Australia, retrieved from: http://www.latrobe.edu.au/__data/assets/pdf_file/0005/576554/31631-ARCSHS_NSASSSH_FINAL-A-3.pdf

Chapter 10

1.   Grenoble, R., 'Cop sues Starbucks after spilling free cup of coffee on himself', *Huffington Post*, 9 May 2016, retrieved from: http://www.huffingtonpost.com.au/entry/cop-sues-starbucks-hot-coffee_n_7241360

2.   CBS News, 'Woman hit by car sues Google over directions', 1 June 2010, retrieved from: https://www.cbsnews.com/news/woman-hit-by-car-sues-google-over-directions/

Chapter 11

1.   Lenhart, A., Pew Research Center, 2015, 'Teen, social media and technology overview 2015', retrieved from: http://www.pewinternet.org/2015/04/09/teens-social-media-technology-2015

2.   Madden, M., Lenhart, A., Cortesi, S., Grasser, U., Duggan, M., Smith, M., and Beaton, M., Pew Research Center, 2013, 'Teens, social media, and privacy', retrieved from: http://pewinternet.org/Reports/2013/Teens-Social-Media-And-Privacy.aspx

3.	Rideout, V., Common Sense Media, 'The common sense census: Media use by tweens and teens', 2015, retrieved from: https://www.commonsensemedia.org/research/the-common-sense-census-media-use-by-tweens-and-teens

4.	Australian Psychological Society, 'Stress and wellbeing: How Australians are coping with life. The findings of the Australian Psychological Society Stress and Wellbeing in Australia Survey 2015', retrieved from: https://www.psychology.org.au/Assets/Files/PW15-SR.pdf

5.	Australian Psychological Society, 'Stress and wellbeing: How Australians are coping with life. The findings of the Australian Psychological Society Stress and Wellbeing in Australia Survey 2015', retrieved from: https://www.psychology.org.au/Assets/Files/PW15-SR.pdf

Chapter 12

1.	Lawrence, D., Johnson, S., Hafekost, J., Boterhoven De Haan, K., Sawyer, M., Ainley, J., and Zubrick, S.R., 2015, 'The mental health of children and adolescents: Report on the second Australian child and adolescent survey of mental health and wellbeing', Department of Health, Canberra, retrieved from: https://www.health.gov.au/internet/main/publishing.nsf/Content/9DA8CA21306FE6EDCA257E2700016945/%24File/child2.pdf

2.	Mojtabai, R., Olfson, M., and Han, B., 2016, 'National trends in the prevalence and treatment of depression in adolescents and young adults', *Pediatrics*, retrieved from: http://pediatrics.aappublications.org/content/pediatrics/138/6/e20161878.full.pdf

Chapter 13

1.	Lawrence, D., Johnson, S., Hafekost, J., Boterhoven De Haan, K., Sawyer, M., Ainley, J., and Zubrick, S.R., 2015, 'The mental health of children and adolescents: Report on the second Australian child and adolescent survey of mental health and wellbeing', Department of Health, Canberra, retrieved from: https://www.health.gov.au/internet/main/publishing.nsf/Content/9DA8CA21306FE6EDCA257E2700016945/%24File/child2.pdf

2.   Campbell, D., 'NHS figures show "shocking" rise in self-harm among young', *The Guardian*, 24 October 2016, retrieved from: https://www.theguardian.com/society/2016/oct/23/nhs-figures-show-shocking-rise-self-harm-young-people

3.   Morgan, C., Webb, R.T., Carr, M.J., Kontopantelis, E., Green, J., Chew-Graham, C.A., Kapur, N., and Ashcroft, D.M., 2017, 'Incidence, clinical management, and mortality risk following self-harm among children and adolescents: Cohort study in primary care', *British Medical Journal*, retrieved from: http://www.bmj.com/content/359/bmj.j4351.long

INDEX